gluten free
EVERY DAY
COOKBOOK

gluten free
EVERY DAY
COOKBOOK

MORE THAN 100 EASY AND DELICIOUS RECIPES FROM THE GLUTEN-FREE CHEF

ROBERT M. LANDOLPHI

Andrews McMeel Publishing, LLC

Kansas City

09 10 11 12 13 RR2 10 9 8 7 6 5 4 3

Library of Congress Cataloging-in-Publication Data

Landolphi, Robert M.
  Gluten free every day cookbook : more than 100 easy and delicious recipes from the gluten-free chef / Robert M. Landolphi.
      p. cm.
  Includes index.
  ISBN-13: 978-0-7407-7813-1
  ISBN-10: 0-7407-7813-7
  1. Gluten-free diet—Recipes. I. Title.

RM237.86.L355 2009
641.5'638—dc22

                                                2008046951

Design and composition by Delsie Chambon

www.andrewsmcmeel.com

This book is dedicated to my
beautiful wife, Angela.

CONTENTS

FOREWORD

Congratulations! You are about to embark on the gluten-free diet, a healthy lifestyle that eliminates many of the unnecessary refined carbohydrates found in the normal American diet. The gluten-free diet is designed to remove the obvious sources of wheat in our desserts, fried and processed foods, breads, cereals, and pastas, as well as the hidden wheat sources found in such items as soups, coatings and flavorings, some brands of blue cheese, and so on. Of course, a gluten-free diet also eliminates other grains that contain gluten, such as barley (including malt), rye, and any cross-contaminated oats.

A diagnosis of celiac disease is one of the major factors behind the gluten-free journey. However, many people also suffer from an undiagnosed gluten intolerance, whereas others simply feel better when not eating wheat. There are also many others who just want to reduce their intake of refined wheat flour and who therefore heartily and joyfully embrace the gluten-free lifestyle. Celiac disease itself is a disease of intestinal malabsorption, which manifests in a number of nutritional deficiencies leading to a variety of painful and dangerous symptoms. These deficiencies and symptoms are noticeably corrected when all gluten is removed from the diet and is replaced by the proper sources of protein, fruits, vegetables, allowable whole grains and carbohydrates, dairy products, and healthful fats.

A gluten-free diet does not have to be bland or boring, nor does this diet mean that you have to starve yourself or deprive yourself of the foods you love. All you have to do is to walk into a health foods store or even some local supermarkets to find gluten-free pastas, breads, muffins, prepared meals, cereals, pizzas, desserts, snacks, and even beer. Gluten-free restaurants, bakeries, and cruises are now available. And whatever foods you can't find close to home can always be found on the Internet. There exists today a comparable substitute for nearly any food or recipe you love to make or eat, but feel that you have to give up because it contains gluten. As long as the proper ingredients and cooking techniques are used, your recipe will work. This discovery can be fun, especially for the well-seasoned cook, or even for the novice willing to give it a try.

Regardless of whether you do or do not have celiac disease, at different ages and stages in our lives we require varying amounts of nutrients, total calories, fiber, vitamins, and minerals, and even different sources and percentages from which they are derived. Calories come from carbohydrates, proteins, fats, and alcohol. There are no other sources of calories. To achieve good health, to grow or repair or heal or just to maintain proper body dynamics, we must become aware of what to eat, how much to eat, and how to strike the proper balance of nutrients. *Gluten Free Every Day Cookbook* will help you on this journey.

Congratulations, again! You are holding on to a book that will bring enormous pleasure to your gluten-free life. Using *Gluten Free Every Day Cookbook*'s recipes, you and your family and friends will enjoy easy and delectable dishes ranging from soups to entrées to desserts. I recommend that you try them all. They have been tested and perfected by a chef whose wife and several extended family members require a totally gluten-free diet, and whose dinner guests consistently rave about everything he prepares—very often unaware that they are eating a gluten-free meal!

Always remember that balance is an important component in the gluten-free diet. This means discovering, preparing, and eating the best proteins (meat, poultry, eggs, fish, beans, and legumes), fruits and vegetables (which are good sources of antioxidants, phytochemicals, fiber, vitamins, and minerals), calcium, whole grains, nuts, and proper fats. This approach can lead to a healthy heart and clear skin, strong bones and muscles, and properly functioning nervous and metabolic systems, resulting in a longer, happier life.

One final note: Balance also includes the occasional splurge. Whether it's needed to increase calories, to squelch a craving, or just to indulge in its sheer gastronomic pleasure, you can have that delicious piece of Bittersweet Chocolate–Walnut Cake, slice of Blaspberry Pie, or chunk of Nutty Brittle on the gluten-free diet—most especially enjoyable when prepared the Gluten-Free Chef's incredible way!

Bon appétit!

—Elizabeth A. FitzGerald, RD, CD-N

ACKNOWLEDGMENTS

This book is a milestone in an incredible journey, one that required the assistance and support of many good people. I want to take this opportunity to thank my wife, Angela, because after hearing her say about three million times, "You should write a cookbook," I actually wrote a cookbook. Angela's patience, encouragement, and input are the underpinnings of this manuscript.

My gratitude is also due to Elizabeth FitzGerald, registered dietitian, who spent countless hours researching nutritional information on new products and flours, and passionately shared her wealth of knowledge regarding celiac disease and the gluten-free diet. Loving thanks to the members of my family and all of my friends who shared recipes, endured taste tests, and gave honest opinions when I needed them most. To my brother-in-law, Kevin, whose heartfelt response when trying each new dish was, "This is awesome": Your kudos kept me going. I send my appreciation to Wally Lamb, novelist and friend, for his advice, guidance, and direction at several points along the way. Also, I thank James Haller, cookbook author, for sharing his publishing experiences and suggestions, which eventually led me to find my literary agent, Mary Beth Chappell. I want to thank her for her honesty and fairness, and for believing in the potential for this project. To my editor, Lane Butler, thank you for bringing it all to fruition. Finally, from the depths of my heart, I prayerfully thank the Lord for once again showing me that the fruit of all suffering is always a greater good, and that it typically results in abundant blessings. I thank Him for everything and everyone He has so generously sent into my life.

INTRODUCTION

This book is the culmination of a personal journey that included years of trials, disappointments, research, and joy. It is geared toward a specific and ever-increasing population, the wheat- and gluten-intolerant, and it comes with a very personal and intriguing story.

In 1996, I married a young, bright, enthusiastic woman and we began planning for a hopeful future and a large family. It soon became clear, however, that we were not completely in control of our destiny. While she was in graduate school, Angela's health took a slow but progressive turn for the worse. After several months of fatigue, digestive symptoms, and unexplained aches and pains, even more symptoms emerged: rashes, hair loss, peripheral neuropathies (tingling in fingers/toes), muscle weakness, numbness and pain, and headaches, and then a complete shutdown of her reproductive system. Countless doctor visits with numerous specialists followed. Their diagnoses included Epstein-Barr virus, chronic fatigue syndrome, undetectable Lyme disease, adrenal dysfunction, and multiple sclerosis, yet no tests were conclusive. Angela continued to work and to plod through each day, but she was beginning to forget what it felt like to be "well." Some days were so bad that she opted to take out life insurance at the age of twenty-nine. Instead of planning for a baby and decorating a nursery, we began contemplating her seemingly eventual funeral. After she had suffered for almost three years, a family member sent us an article detailing a digestive disorder called celiac disease. That started the ball rolling.

Celiac disease, as explained by Peter H. R. Green, M.D., director of the Celiac Disease Center at Columbia University, is a multisystem disorder that begins in the small intestine. The disease is triggered by gluten, the primary protein found in wheat, barley, and rye grains, which causes an immune inflammatory response in the cells that line the small intestine and results in the flattening of the intestinal villa. The damage caused in the small intestine renders the body unable to absorb nutrients properly, causing a general malabsorption that leads to varied and complex physical symptoms. Celiac disease is now considered one of the most common and underdiagnosed hereditary autoimmune disorders in the United States. Treatment is easy: no medicine, no therapy, just strict lifelong adherence to a gluten-free diet.

This sounded simple enough, so Angela decided to give it a try. Day one without bread, pasta, cereal, pastries, cake, muffins, and so on wasn't too bad, and so she began day two similarly, with eggs and bacon for breakfast, chicken and carrots for lunch, and grilled fish, baked potato, and beans for dinner. As early as day two on the diet, the symptoms began disappearing. By days three and four, there was no going back: the headaches were gone, the numbness had ended, digestion was normal, her fingernails began growing, and her spirits were lifting. Within three months of no gluten, her gut and body were healing and the hormones that had shut down were beginning to be produced again. It became clear that Angela had adult-onset celiac disease, and our hope of resuming normal life activities, and of one day having a family, was back on the horizon. It did, however, take nearly four years of strict adherence to the gluten-free lifestyle (along with the prayers of our priests and our friends) to finally conceive, but with no doctors and no drugs involved! And so, every day we revel in our beautiful, healthy young sons, Joseph Anthony and Andrew Robert.

Angela has always said that she doesn't miss gluten, and that nothing could taste good enough to make her want to ingest it again. But I couldn't help but notice her wistful look when we passed by a bakery, or when various dishes like certain soups or pasta dishes arrived in a restaurant, or at Thanksgiving dinner when Grandma dished out the stuffing. Once in a while I heard, "Gee, that banana bread smells great," or "I wish I could have a bowl of clam chowder," and "Remember when I could eat chocolate cream pie?" And so, with a lifelong love of cooking, a culinary arts degree from Johnson and Wales University, and the desire to create good gluten-free meals and desserts to keep my wife healthy, I dove into experimenting. Using various combinations of chestnut, sorghum, tapioca, corn, and rice flours, as well as many of the gluten-free products on the market today, I began to develop a repertoire of dishes that Angela could eat. I eventually began conducting gluten-free cooking demonstrations for support groups, friends, and natural foods stores such as Wild Oats and Whole Foods. At the demos, I often posed the question to those in the crowd: If I were to create a cookbook, what kinds of dishes would you be interested in making? "We want to know everything—how to make easy soups, appetizers, entrées, and desserts!" was always the answer.

Gluten Free Every Day Cookbook is truly a labor of love: my love for the culinary arts; my love for my wife and my desire for her to stay healthy, strong, and happy; and a deep and resounding love for our children. Perhaps our boys are the real inspiration, for without the existence of a gluten-free diet for their mother, they may never have been conceived.

And so it is with hope and pride that I share this story, a number of our favorite recipes, and some invaluable information that I have learned along the way. The recipes have been tried, tested, and tweaked by my best critics, including those with and without gluten intolerance. This has been a personal goal: that any person tasting these dishes would not even notice that they are gluten free.

This book contains recipes for fabulous baked dishes, including White Chocolate–Strawberry Pie, Almond Biscotti, and Bittersweet Chocolate–Walnut Cake, along with soups such as Corn, Potato, and Leek Chowder and Chocolate-Espresso Chili. The recipes for entrées are varied and interesting, such as Hazelnut-Encrusted Salmon with Cilantro-Lime Crème, Shrimp and Vegetable Pad Thai, and Chicken Enchilada Casserole; and among the side dishes are Tri-Spiced Onion Rings, Smoked Gouda Polenta, and Candied Sweet Potatoes. The book also contains glossaries and information about essential ingredients and techniques, as well as tips for eating away from home.

I hope you will enjoy reading and using this book as much as I enjoyed creating it.

Mangia, mangia!

CHAPTER 1

GLUTEN-FREE
BASICS

Flours
Starches
Nut Meals
Seeds

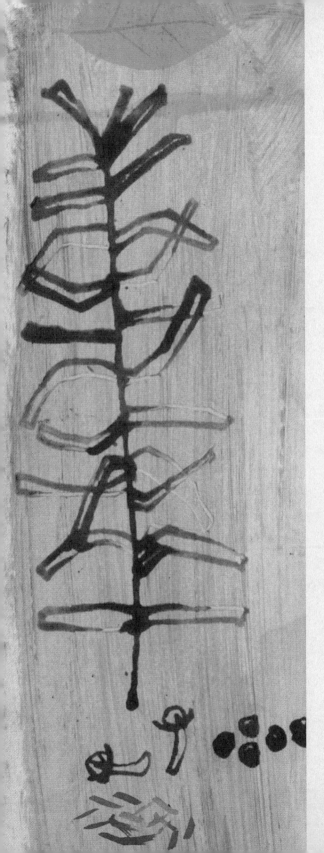

GLUTEN-FREE FLOURS, STARCHES, NUT MEALS, AND SEEDS

Flours and Starches

Flour is made from finely milled wheat or other grains or food products. If the average person were asked, "What is flour made from?" most would answer, "Wheat." Not a surprising response, given that during most of our lives we have been fed and consumed large quantities of wheat flour in a multitude of forms. Most people don't realize that there are many other tasty and healthy flours, made from other grains and foods that do not contain gluten.

When giving a cooking demonstration, I also typically ask the participants to describe the flavor of flour. After some thought, most will reply that flour doesn't taste like anything. And that, of course, is right. Refined white wheat flour has almost no flavor of its own. The herbs, spices, and other ingredients that are incorporated into it provide the flavor. Plain white rice flour, cornstarch, and tapioca flour have the same bland, flavorless taste. On the other hand, whole-wheat flour has a grainier, nuttier taste, as do whole-grain brown rice flour and soy flours. Therefore, when starting out with gluten-free baking, I always suggest experimenting to find a flour that is most similar to what you normally use. There are also some very good gluten-free flour mixes on the market today, which are convenient and help save time in the kitchen. However, it is important to note that the mix that makes a great cake probably won't make a very good pizza crust. The recipes in this book have been created to yield the best results with combinations of nongluten flours and or thickeners, and will add many gems to your gluten-free treasure chest. Creating the perfect blend of flours often requires mixing the right proportions of both whole-grain and refined flours. While there are always exceptions in recipes due to flavor profiles and textures, the importance of eating whole grains, with their valuable vitamins, minerals, and fiber, cannot be stressed enough. Examples of these whole grains include brown rice, amaranth, cornmeal, oatmeal, quinoa, sorghum, and teff.

Numerous gluten-free flours are available on the market today, with new varieties and choices being developed every year. And the only way to become familiar with all their flavor and texture profiles is to dig in and experiment. In this chapter, you will find a list of different gluten-free flours, a description of their tastes, an explanation of how they are best used, a list of their nutritional values, and the proper storage techniques needed for each. This list is a guide— and no one will ever have them all on hand at any given time. The flours and starches that I use most often and find to be the most versatile are brown and white rice flours, sorghum flour, tapioca flour, potato starch, and cornstarch. Sweet rice flour, soy flour, quinoa flour, nut flours, and other miscellaneous flours make up my secondary stock. In addition, xanthan gum is always available in my pantry—a must-have for gluten-free baking in any venue.

When substituting gluten-free flours, consider the density of each type of flour. The lighter, starchier flours such as corn, potato, tapioca, and arrowroot are easily interchangeable, and will yield a lighter, fluffier texture to the finished baked item. Heavier, denser flours such as rice, sorghum, and chickpea can be substituted for one another and will result in a more weighty and dense final product. Another consideration is the targeted flavor profile. For example, chickpea flour has a much stronger taste than brown rice flour, which will be reflected in the finished cake, cookie, or sweet bar. Other flours such as coconut or nut meal flours should only be used in small amounts to add flavor, and should not be used solely on their own.

When following a recipe that normally calls for wheat flour, combine 2/3 cup heavier, denser gluten-free flours with 1/3 cup lighter, starchier flours, and substitute this blend for each cup of wheat flour. After trying the finished product, make adjustments according to preference with regard to taste, texture, and color.

Amaranth flour: Made from tiny seeds that are ground into a light brown flour with a nutty and peppery flavor. Can be used as a thickener in gravies and soups, or as a flavor enhancer when mixed with other baking flours.

Store in an airtight container in a cool, dry place for up to 1 month, refrigerate for up to 6 months, or freeze for up to 1 year.

Nutritional information per 1/4 cup (30 g) = 110 calories, 18 calories from fat, 2 g total fat, 0.50 g saturated fat, 0 g trans fat, 0 g cholesterol, 6 mg sodium, 20 g total carbohydrate, 3 g dietary fiber, 0 g sugars, 4 g protein

Arrowroot starch: A white, powdery, tasteless flour derived from the dried root stalks of a tropical tuber. Can be used as a substitute for cornstarch when cooking or baking.

Store in an airtight container in a cool, dry place for up to 3 months, refrigerate for up to 1 year, or freeze for up to 2 years.

Nutritional information per 1/4 cup (32 g): 110 calories, 0 calories from fat, 0 g total fat, 0 g saturated fat, 0 g trans fat, 0 mg cholesterol, 0 mg sodium, 28 g total carbohydrate, 1 g dietary fiber, 0 g sugars, 0 g protein

Black bean flour: Black beans are small beans with a cream-colored flesh and black skin. The flour tends to be grainy in texture and has a strong flavor that can overpower milder flours. Black bean flour can be used in Mexican dips, veggie burgers, soups, stews, and tortillas.

Store in an airtight container in the refrigerator for up to 6 months, or freeze for up to 1 year.

Nutritional information per 1/4 cup (35 g): 120 calories, 0 calories from fat, 0 g total fat, 0 g saturated fat, 0 g trans fat, 0 mg cholesterol, 0 mg sodium, 22 g total carbohydrate, 5 g dietary fiber, 1 g sugars, 8 g protein

Brown rice flour: Has a grainy texture and nutty taste that work exceptionally well in baked goods. In addition, it is high in fiber, vitamins, and minerals.

Store in an airtight container in a cool, dry place for up to 1 month, refrigerate for up to 6 months, or freeze for up to 1 year.

Nutritional information per 1/4 cup (40 g): 140 calories, 10 calories from fat, 1 g total fat, 0 g saturated fat, 0 g trans fat, 0 mg cholesterol, 5 mg sodium, 31 g total carbohydrate, 1 g dietary fiber, 0 g sugars, 3 g protein

Buckwheat flour: Derived not from a grass, but from a plant related to rhubarb. Often used in commercial cereals, it is also ground into a flour for pancakes, waffles, and other baked goods. It has an earthy, sour, and nutty flavor and is very high in fiber, carbohydrates, and minerals.

Store in an airtight container in the refrigerator for up to 4 months, or in the freezer for up to 1 year.

Nutritional information per 1/4 cup (31 g): 100 calories, 8 calories from fat, 1 g total fat, 0 g saturated fat, 0 g trans fat, 0 mg cholesterol, 0 mg sodium, 21 g total carbohydrate, 4 g dietary fiber, 0 g sugars, 4 g protein

Coconut flour: Made from the ground meat of the coconut, it is very high in fiber and protein, and should be blended with other flours to add texture and consistency to baked goods. Flour made from 100 percent organic coconut has a naturally subtle sweetness and wonderfully fresh coconut flavor.

Store in an airtight container refrigerated for up to 12 months, or freeze for up to 2 years.

Nutritional information per 1/4 cup (28 g): 120 calories, 30 calories from fat, 3 g total fat, 2 g saturated fat, 0 g trans fat, 0 mg cholesterol, 0 mg sodium, 20 g total carbohydrate, 12 g dietary fiber, 0 g sugars, 4 g protein

Corn flour: Contains the whole kernel of corn and is ground into a much finer blend than that of cornmeal. Popular types of corn flour are masa harina (ground from the white or yellow corn used to make hominy) and harinilla (made from blue corn and used primarily in Mexican dishes).

Refrigerate for up to 1 year, or freeze for up to 2 years.

Nutritional information per 1/4 cup (29 g): 106 calories, 10 calories from fat, 1 g total fat, 0 g saturated fat, 0 g trans fat, 0 mg cholesterol, 2 mg sodium, 22 g total carbohydrate, 4 g dietary fiber, 0 g sugars, 2 g protein

Cornmeal: Dried corn kernels ground into a meal that is thicker and coarser than corn flour. Best used for making breads, muffins, polenta, and grits, and for encrusting foods. Available in yellow, white, and blue varieties. I prefer stone-ground cornmeal.

Store in an airtight container in a cool, dry

place for up to 2 months, refrigerate for up to 6 months, or freeze for up to 1 year.

Nutritional information per 1/4 cup (33 g) medium grind: 110 calories, 10 calories from fat, 1 g total fat, 0 g saturated fat, 0 g trans fat, 0 mg cholesterol, 10 mg sodium, 23 g total carbohydrate, 5 g dietary fiber, 0 g sugars, 2 g protein

Cornstarch: A fine white powder milled from corn and primarily used as a thickener. When blended with other gluten-free flours, it can be used to make baked goods or crisp coating for meats and vegetables. Its mild taste makes it a perfect vehicle for other ingredients.

Store indefinitely in an airtight container in a cool, dry place.

Nutritional information per tablespoon (8 g): 30 calories, 0 calories from fat, 0 g total fat, 0 g saturated fat, 0 g trans fat, 0 mg cholesterol, 0 mg sodium, 7 g total carbohydrate, 0 g dietary fiber, 0 g sugars, 0 g protein

Fava bean flour: Dried favas are skinned and milled into a fine-textured flour with a slightly bitter taste. Because of its assertive taste, this flour should be blended in small amounts with other gluten-free flours in baked goods such as quick breads.

Store in an airtight container in the refrigerator for up to 6 months, or freeze for up to 1 year.

Nutritional information per 1/4 cup (33 g): 110 calories, 5 calories from fat, 0.5 g total fat, 0 g saturated fat, 0 g trans fat, 0 mg cholesterol, 0 mg sodium, 19 g total carbohydrate, 8 g dietary fiber, 1 g sugars, 9 g protein

Garbanzo (chickpea) flour: Garbanzos, or chickpeas, are processed into a very fine flour with a rich, sweet, and nutty flavor. Also called besan flour, it is a staple ingredient in many dishes from India, North Africa, and the Middle East, such as the Indian *cheela ka besan*, a thin pancake eaten like pita bread. Use to blend with other gluten-free flours, and as a binder in bean or veggie burgers.

Store in an airtight container in the refrigerator for up to 6 months, or freeze for up to 1 year.

Nutritional information per 1/4 cup (30 g): 110 calories, 15 calories from fat, 2 g total fat, 0 g saturated fat, 0 g trans fat, 0 mg cholesterol, 5 mg sodium, 18 g total carbohydrate, 5 g dietary fiber, 3 g sugars, 6 g protein

Millet flour: Derived from a highly nutritious and versatile grain, this flour is mildly sweet, with a nutty flavor. When blended with other gluten-free flours, it results in lighter baked goods. Try adding millet flour to pancakes, scones, cookies, or quick breads.

Store in an airtight container in a cool, dry place for up to 1 month, refrigerate for up to 3 months, or freeze for up to 6 months.

Nutritional information per 1/4 cup (30 g): 110 calories, 11 calories from fat, 1 g total fat, 0 g saturated fat, 0 g trans fat, 0 mg cholesterol, 2 mg sodium, 22 g total carbohydrate, 4 g dietary fiber, 0 g sugars, 3 g protein

Oat flour: You can purchase gluten-free oat flour, or make your own by processing rolled oats in a food processor or blender. Oats can pose a problem for people with celiac disease, due to issues with cross-contamination.

However, a few companies, such as Cream Hill Estates, Bob's Red Mill, and Gluten Free Oats, are dedicated to growing, producing and packaging noncontaminated oats. These companies produce steel-cut and old-fashioned oats that are certified gluten-free. Oat flour adds flavor and texture to baked goods, and can be used to bind meat loaf.

Store in an airtight container in a cool, dry place for up to 3 months, refrigerate for up to 6 months, or freeze for up to 1 year.

Nutritional information per 1/4 cup (30 g): 120 calories, 19 calories from fat, 2 g total fat, 0.35 g saturated fat, 0 mg cholesterol, 0 mg sodium, 19 g total carbohydrate, 3 g dietary fiber, 0 g sugars, 5 g protein

Green pea flour: Split pea flours come in yellow or green varieties and have a slightly sweet flavor and a powdery texture. They can be used to make a creamy pea soup or added in small amounts to guacamole, cookies, and muffins.

Store in an airtight container in the refrigerator for up to 6 months, or freeze for up to 1 year.

Nutritional information per 1/4 cup (40 g): 133 calories, 0 calories from fat, 0 g total fat, 0 g saturated fat, 0 g trans fat, 0 mg cholesterol, 5 mg sodium, 25 g total carbohydrate, 11 g dietary fiber, 3 g sugars, 10 g protein

Potato flour: A light flour milled from cooked, dried potatoes. Used in baked goods, it has a slightly chalky taste and starchy texture.

Store indefinitely in an airtight container in a cool, dry place.

Nutritional information per 1/4 cup (45 g): 160 calories, 6 calories from fat, 0.66 g total fat, 0 g saturated fat, 0 g trans fat, 0 mg cholesterol, 13 mg sodium, 36 g total carbohydrate, 2 g dietary fiber, 0 g sugars, 4 g protein

Potato starch: A flour derived from cooked potatoes that are washed until just the starch remains. Used as a thickener, as well as an ingredient in many baked goods. Potato starch and potato flour are not interchangeable.

Store indefinitely in an airtight container in a cool, dry place.

Nutritional information per 1/4 cup (48 g): 160 calories, 0 calories from fat, 0 g total fat, 0 g saturated fat, 0 g trans fat, 0 mg cholesterol, 0 mg sodium, 40 g total carbohydrate, 0 g dietary fiber, 0 g sugars, 0 g protein

Quinoa (pronounced keen-wa) flour: Ground from a seed, this flour has a slightly nutty flavor. It can be used in baked goods (such as cookies and cakes) to help retain moisture.

Store in an airtight container in the refrigerator for up to 6 months, or freeze for up to 1 year.

Nutritional information per 1/4 cup (28 g): 120 calories, 15 calories from fat, 2 g total fat, 0 g saturated fat, 0 g trans fat, 0 mg cholesterol, 8 mg sodium, 21 g total carbohydrate, 4 g dietary fiber, 0 g sugars, 4 g protein

Sorghum flour: A heavy flour ground from a cereal grain, sorghum flour resembles wheat flour and works very well in baked goods such as muffins and breads.

Store in an airtight container in a cool, dry

place for up to 1 month, refrigerate for up to 3 months, or freeze for up to 6 months.

Nutritional information per 1/4 cup (34 g): 120 calories, 10 calories from fat, 1 g total fat, 0 g saturated fat, 0 g trans fat, 0 mg cholesterol, 0 mg sodium, 25 g total carbohydrate, 3 g dietary fiber, 0 g sugars, 4 g protein

Soy flour: Made from finely ground roasted soybeans, this flour has a grainy texture and a nutty flavor and is usually combined with other flours for baking or coating. It contains all the amino acids needed to make a complete protein.

Store in an airtight container in the refrigerator for up to 6 months, or freeze for up to 1 year.

Nutritional information per 1/4 cup (28 g): 120 calories, 50 calories from fat, 6 g total fat, 1 g saturated fat, 0 g trans fat, 0 mg cholesterol, 0 mg sodium, 8 g total carbohydrate, 3 g dietary fiber, 2 g sugars, 10 g protein

Sweet potato flour: A white flour with a sweet flavor and stiff texture, derived from white sweet potatoes. Use in making muffins, breads, biscuits, and cakes.

Nutritional information per 1/4 cup (45 g): 120 calories, 9 calories from fat, 1 g total fat, 0 g saturated fat, 0 g cholesterol, 160 mg sodium, 34 g total carbohydrate, 6 g dietary fiber, 0 g sugars, 1 g protein

Sweet rice flour: Also known as glutinous rice flour because of its starchy properties, this flour gives baked goods a nice, chewy texture made from high-starch, short-grain rice. Sweet rice flour and white rice flour are not interchangeable.

Store in an airtight container in a cool, dry place for up to 1 year.

Nutritional information per 1/4 cup (51 g): 180 calories, 5 calories from fat, 0.5 g total fat, 0 g saturated fat, 0 g trans fat, 0 mg cholesterol, 0 mg sodium, 40 g total carbohydrate, 1 g dietary fiber, 1 g sugars, 3 g protein

Tapioca flour: Derived from the root of the cassava plant, this flour is very light, powdery, smooth, and tasteless. It can be used as a thickening agent, as well as combined with other gluten-free flours to make delicious baked goods.

Store indefinitely in an airtight container in a cool, dry place.

Nutritional information per 1/4 cup (30 g): 100 calories, 0 calories from fat, 0 g total fat, 0 g saturated fat, 0 g trans fat, 0 mg cholesterol, 0 mg sodium, 26 g total carbohydrate, 0 g dietary fiber, 0 g sugars, 0 g protein

Teff flour: Made from small seeds that are ground to a soft and porous flour. It has a slight molasses flavor and may be substituted for other seeds and grains in baked goods.

Store in an airtight container in a cool, dry place for up to 1 month, refrigerate for up to 3 months, or freeze for up to 6 months.

Nutritional information per 1/4 cup (30 g): 113 calories, 5 calories from fat, 1 g total fat, 0 g saturated fat, 0 g trans fat, 0 mg cholesterol, 5 mg sodium, 22 g total carbohydrate, 4 g dietary fiber, 0 g sugars, 4 g protein

White bean flour: A mild-flavored flour that adds fiber to baked goods, and can be mixed with warm water or stews to make a creamy soup or gravy.

Store in an airtight container in the refrigerator for up to 6 months, or freeze for up to 1 year.

Nutritional information per 1/4 cup (32 g): 110 calories, 0 calories from fat, 0 g saturated fat, 0 g trans fat, 0 mg cholesterol, 0 mg sodium, 20 g total carbohydrate, 8 g dietary fiber, 2 g sugars, 7 g protein

White rice flour: Made from white rice ground into a powdery, tasteless flour. Usually combined with other gluten-free flours when used in preparing muffins, breads, and other baked goods.

Store indefinitely in an airtight container in a cool, dry place.

Nutritional information per 1/4 cup (40 g): 150 calories, 5 calories from fat, 0.5 g total fat, 0 g saturated fat, 0 g trans fat, 0 mg cholesterol, 0 mg sodium, 32 g total carbohydrate, 1 g dietary fiber, 0 g sugars, 2 g protein

Xanthan gum: Xanthan gum is a white powdery flour, produced from the fermentation of corn sugar, which is used as a thickener or binding agent for gluten-free baked goods. It is also used as an emulsifier in many sauces and salad dressings—a must-have in the gluten-free household.

Store in an airtight container in a cool, dry place indefinitely.

Nutritional information per 1 tablespoon (9 g): 30 calories, 0 calories from fat, 0 g total fat, 0 g saturated fat, 0 g trans

fat, 0 mg cholesterol, 10 mg sodium, 7 g total carbohydrate, 7 g dietary fiber, 0 g sugar, 0 g protein

Nut Meals\Flours

Nut flours are ground from the cake or
meat of the nut, after the oils are pressed out;
whereas nut meals are ground from the whole
nuts, making them oilier and coarser. Nut
flours and meals add fiber, protein, and flavor
to a variety of dishes.

Almond meal flour: High in fiber and calcium, and rich in antioxidants and phosphorus.
Blend almond meal flour with other gluten-free
flours to create nutty flavored cakes, cookies,
muffins or shortbreads. I like adding a small
amount of almond meal flour to my pastry
crusts for an additional rich and nutty flavor.

Store in an airtight container in the refrigerator for up to 6 months, or freeze for up to 1 year.

*Nutritional information per 1/4 cup (28 g): 160 calories,
120 calories from fat, 14 g total fat, 1 g saturated fat,
0 g trans fat, 0 mg cholesterol, 10 mg sodium, 6 g total
carbohydrate, 3 g dietary fiber, 1 g sugars, 6 g protein*

Chestnut flour: Unlike other nuts, chestnuts
are very low in fat and very high in complex
carbohydrates and protein. They have been
called the "grain that grows on trees," and have
a mellow, sweet flavor. Chestnut flour is used in
breads, cakes, and muffins.

Store in an airtight container in a cool, dry
place for up to 1 month, refrigerate for up to
6 months, or freeze for up to 1 year.

*Nutritional information per 1/4 cup (25 g): 90 calories,
10 calories from fat, 1 g total fat, 0 g saturated fat,
0 mg cholesterol, 10 mg sodium, 20 g total carbohydrate,
0 g dietary fiber, 0 g sugars, 1 g protein*

Hazelnut meal flour: High in fiber, folate,
vitamin E, and other antioxidants. It is made from
pure ground hazelnuts and adds a rich flavor to
baked goods such as breads, muffins, and cakes.

Store in an airtight container in the refrigerator
for up to 6 months, or freeze for up to 1 year.

*Nutritional information per 1/4 cup (28 g): 180 calories,
150 calories from fat, 17 g total fat, 1 g saturated fat,
0 g trans fat, 0 mg cholesterol, 5 g total carbohydrate,
3 g dietary fiber, 1 g sugars, 4 g protein*

Peanut flour (defatted): Peanut flour comes
from peanuts that are lightly roasted and
ground. "Defatted" means the peanuts have
gone through a process to remove their oil. The
result is a high-protein, low-fat flour useful for
cooking. It should be used blended with other
gluten-free flours in baking. Peanut flour can be
used in baked goods such as cookies and breads
or blended with other gluten-free flours for
coating chicken, beef, or pork. Try adding it to
chilis or stews to provide a rich, nutty flavor.

Store in an airtight container in a refrigerator
for up to 6 months, or freeze for up to 1 year.

*Nutritional information per 1/4 cup (15 g): 49 calories,
0 calories from fat, 0 g total fat, 0 g saturated fat,
0 mg cholesterol, 27 mg sodium, 5 g total carbohydrate,
2 g dietary fiber, 1 g sugars, 8 g protein*

Nuts and Seeds

Nuts and seeds have been a nutritious food for thousands of years. They can be purchased either in or out of the shell, whole, halved, sliced, chopped, raw, or roasted. You will find that the addition of nuts and seeds to your dishes will add texture, moisture, and most important, great flavor.

Flaxseed meal: Flaxseed meal can be purchased in a whole, ground, cracked, or oil form. (The oil is typically served cold on salads as dressings and does not heat well in baking or cooking.) Ground flaxseeds have a velvety soft texture and a slightly nutty flavor. They can be used as a thickener for soups or stews, as a binder for coating proteins such as chicken or fish, and in baked goods such as muffins and breads.

When adding flaxseed meal to baked goods, it is always a good idea to use small quantities and to blend it with other flours. Flaxseed meal contains a great deal of natural oil that can overpower the flavor of a dish when used in large quantities. I use golden milled flaxseeds in my Pecorino Romano Pizza Crust to give it a hearty, rich, and nutty flavor.

Store in an airtight container in a refrigerator for 6 months to 1 year.

Nutritional information per 2 tablespoons (13 g) ground: 60 calories, 40 calories from fat, 4.5 g total fat, 0 g saturated fat, 0 g trans fat, 0 mg cholesterol, 0 mg sodium, 4 g total carbohydrate, 4 g dietary fiber, 0 g sugars, 3 g protein

Hazelnuts: Also known as the filbert, has a rich and earthy flavor that works well in baked goods, stews, stuffings, and salads. They can also be used for encrusting fish, beef, poultry or lamb. Try toasting hazelnuts (page 28) to bring out a smoky, subtle sweet flavor.

Store in an airtight container in a refrigerator for up to 6 months or freeze up to 1 year.

Nutritional information per 1/4 cup (30 g): 180 calories, 150 calories from fat, 16 g total fat, 1 g saturated fat, 0 mg cholesterol, 0 mg sodium, 5 g total carbohydrate, 4 g dietary fiber, 1 g sugars, 5 g protein

Macadamia nuts (dry roasted, no salt): Low in sodium, and high in protein, vitamins, minerals, fiber, and antioxidants.

Store in an airtight container in a refrigerator for up to 6 months or freeze up to 1 year.

Nutritional information per 1/4 cup (30 g): 210 calories, 200 calories from fat, 23 g total fat, 3 g saturated fat, 0 mg cholesterol, 0 mg sodium, 4 g total carbohydrate, 2 g dietary fiber, 1 g sugars, 3 g protein

Pecans (raw): A good source of fiber, vitamin E, thiamin, magnesium, and copper. For instructions on toasting pecans, see page 27.

Store in an airtight container in a refrigerator for up to 6 months or freeze up to 1 year.

Nutritional information per 1/4 cup (28 g): 193 calories, 181 calories from fat, 20.2 g total fat, 1.7 g saturated fat, 0 mg cholesterol, 0 mg sodium, 3.9 g total carbohydrate, 2.7 g dietary fiber, 2.6 g sugars, 2.5 g protein

Pine nuts (raw): Edible seeds from pine trees that have a soft texture and buttery flavor. Pine nuts can be toasted (page 27), roasted, eaten whole, or ground into a paste. They are nutritionally rich in essential amino acids and proteins.

Store in an airtight container in a refrigerator for up to 1 month or freeze up to 3 months.

Nutritional information per 1/4 cup (30 g): 220 calories, 190 calories from fat, 21 g total fat, 5 g saturated fat, 0 mg cholesterol, 5 mg sodium, 1 g total carbohydrate, 1 g dietary fiber, 4 g sugars, 6 g protein

Poppy seeds: Poppy seeds are tiny blue-gray seeds that have a nutty aroma and taste. Poppy seeds add flavor and texture to cookies, cakes, and breads, as well as to beef, chicken, pork, fish, and noodle dishes.

Store in an airtight container in a cool, dry place for 3 months, in a refrigerator for 6 months, or in a freezer for 1 year.

Nutritional information per 3 tablespoons (29 g): 170 calories, 120 calories from fat, 14 g total fat, 1.5 g saturated fat, 0 g trans fat, 0 mg cholesterol, 0 mg sodium, 6 g total carbohydrate, 3 g dietary fiber, 0 g sugars, 6 g protein

Pumpkin seeds: Pumpkin seeds are flattish, oval seeds that come from the center of a pumpkin. They are often used in Mexican dishes to assist in thickening sauces. Pumpkin seeds are available in raw or roasted forms. Roasted pumpkin seeds have a wonderful nutty flavor and make a very healthy snack.

Storage in an airtight container in the refrigerator for 6 months or in the freezer for 1 year.

Nutritional information per 3 tablespoons (23 g): 190 calories, 150 calories from fat, 16 g total fat, 2.5 g saturated fat, 0 g trans fat, 0 mg cholesterol, 5 mg sodium, 4 g total carbohydrate, 1 g dietary fiber, 0 g sugars, 8 g protein

Sesame seeds: Sesame seeds can be used as whole seeds sprinkled on top of cooked or baked dishes, or ground and mixed with other gluten-free flours. For more on sesame seeds, see page 27.

Store in an airtight container in a cool, dry place for 3 months, in a refrigerator for 6 months, or in a freezer for 1 year.

Nutritional information per 3 tablespoons (24 g): 160 calories, 122 calories from fat, 13.6 g total fat, 1.9 g saturated fat, 0 mg cholesterol, 3 mg sodium, 7.3 g total carbohydrate, 4 g dietary fiber, 0 g sugars, 4 g protein

Sunflower seeds (hulled and dry roasted): Dried seeds from the sunflower plant that are sold shelled or unshelled, dry or roasted. They can be sprinkled on salads or used in baked goods such as muffins, breads, and cookies.

Storage in an airtight container in a refrigerator for 3 months or in a freezer for 6 months.

Nutritional information per 3 tablespoons (29 g): 143 calories, 101 calories from fat, 11 g total fat, 2 g saturated fat, 0 mg cholesterol, 0 mg sodium, 3 g total carbohydrate, 2 g dietary fiber, 1 g sugars, 7 g protein

Walnuts: Walnuts are very high in omega-3 fatty acids, which assist in lowering cholesterol. They are very versatile, complement both sweet and savory dishes, and can be eaten raw or toasted (page 27).

Store in an airtight container in a refrigerator for up to 6 months or freeze up to 1 year.

Nutritional information per 1/4 cup (30 g): 210 calories, 180 calories from fat, 20 g total fat, 1.5 g saturated fat, 0 mg cholesterol, 0 mg sodium, 3 g total carbohydrate, 3 g dietary fiber, 0 g sugars, 5 g protein

UNDERSTANDING THE RECIPES AND INGREDIENTS

One of the lessons I teach in my university cooking class is called "The Recipe and Its Structure." The focus of that lecture is the importance of understanding what a recipe entails before attempting to prepare it. The following are some simple steps that will make life easier for those learning the nuances of gluten-free cooking, especially when preparing the recipes found in this book.

The first thing I recommend to anyone preparing a new item is to read over the entire recipe, taking into consideration the ingredients, the method of preparation, the time it will take to prepare, the necessary equipment, and the servings the recipe will yield.

When cooking gluten free, sourcing the proper ingredients is of the utmost importance. What I mean by this is it is the chef's responsibility to read every label to make sure that each item contains no wheat, barley, or rye, and that they are also derivative free. Every ingredient found in this cookbook is available in a gluten-free form. Thus, if I list bread crumbs, chicken stock, soy sauce, or crunchy rice cereal in a recipe, always assume that I am referring to a gluten-free product. The bread crumbs must come from gluten-free breads, the stock and soy sauce cannot contain wheat, and the rice cereal should not have any malt flavoring. I will occasionally share the brand name of a particular gluten-free (GF) product that I feel works the best in a particular recipe, or use the GF symbol or ingredient alert as a reminder.

Another tip I share with my students is to begin a recipe by completing any prep work that can be done ahead of time. For example, if a recipe includes 1 cup of toasted walnuts, toast the walnuts and set them aside before jumping into the heart of the recipe. If you know you will need a 1/2 cup chopped onions, chop and cover them until they are added into the skillet or sauce. This will not only save time, but will also help avoid unnecessary mistakes or losing one's place while preparing the recipe, ultimately making the gluten-free cooking experience more enjoyable and successful in the long run.

GLUTEN-FREE KITCHEN EQUIPMENT

As a chef who spends a great deal of time working in commercial kitchens, I have come to rely heavily upon certain key pieces of equipment in an effort to prepare optimal products. The same is true for when I am cooking at home, but on a much smaller scale. While one does not have to run out and purchase every kitchen trinket on the market, it is worthwhile to note that making great tasting, high-quality gluten-free dishes often requires extra steps, procedures, or specific appliances that wouldn't normally be necessary. The following is a list of the pieces of equipment that I feel are essential in the gluten-free kitchen.

Stand mixer: For preparing baked goods, a good-quality electric stand, or heavy-duty, mixer with paddle and whisk attachments for creaming, beating, and whisking is a must. Over the years, my mixer has become a true friend.

Food processor: I could not live without my food processor. I use it for making pastry crusts, pizza dough, coatings for chicken and fish, crumb toppings, and fillings.

Blender: Pie fillings, chowders, bisques, sauces (and the occasional strawberry daiquiri) all require a powerful blender. A food processor may be substituted in many cases, though it is not as efficient.

Knives and cutting boards: Most of the recipes in this book require slicing, dicing, chopping, and/or mincing. Sharp high-quality knives and a large cutting board are important investments for the gluten-free kitchen.

Pots, pans, and mixing bowls: A small arsenal of stockpots, saucepans, muffin tins, bread pans, pie plates, springform pans, cake pans, baking sheets, casserole dishes, and mixing bowls will be necessary for the preparation of the following recipes.

Small tools: Some of the necessary basics include spatulas, ladles, wooden spoons, tongs, ice-cream scoops, measuring spoons, dry measuring cups, liquid measuring cups, a pizza stone, and a sturdy rolling pin.

TOASTING, ROASTING, CARAMELIZING, AND ZESTING

The following techniques will help enhance the flavor and consistency of the crusts, stuffings, coatings, and toppings found in this book.

Toasting Sesame Seeds: In a heavy, dry skillet over medium heat, stir the sesame seeds constantly until they become a shade or two darker than normal.

Toasting Poppy Seeds: In a dry skillet over medium-high heat, stir the poppy seeds for 2 to 3 minutes until fragrant.

Toasting Pine Nuts: In a small sauté pan over low heat, stir the pine nuts constantly until lightly browned, about 5 to 6 minutes. Alternatively, toast them on baking sheet in a preheated 350°F oven for 5 to 6 minutes, or until lightly browned.

Toasting Almonds, Pecans, Walnuts, and Macadamia Nuts: Place the nuts on a baking sheet and toast in a preheated 350°F oven for 12 to 15 minutes, or until lightly browned.

Toasting Hazelnuts: Spread chopped hazelnuts evenly in a dry skillet over medium heat. Stir constantly until toasted, 4 to 5 minutes. Let the hazelnuts cool before being chopped or ground.

Caramelizing Onions: Place 1 tablespoon of olive oil and 1 tablespoon of butter in a sauté pan over medium-low heat. Add the onion and sauté until golden brown.

Roasting Garlic: Place the peeled and sliced garlic cloves in the center of a 12-inch triple-layered foil square. Drizzle olive oil over the top and seal tightly. Roast in a preheated 400°F oven for 30 minutes.

Zesting Citrus Fruit: Zesting is most commonly done with lemons, limes, oranges, and grapefruits to obtain the outer portion of the fruit's peel or rind. It is used to add color, flavor and texture to a recipe. Using a vegetable peeler, hand grater, or zester, cut off or grate only the colored part of the peel, avoiding the bitter white pith. If using a vegetable peeler, mince the zest with a chef's knife.

USING PREPARED GLUTEN-FREE FOODS

Over the past few years, there has been a marked increase in the number of people being diagnosed with celiac disease/gluten intolerance in this country. Accordingly, there has also been an influx of ready-made gluten-free products available in the market. Some are great, but others are not so good. Prepared wheat- and gluten-free foods definitely have a place in a chef's kitchen, but it's important to know how to choose the right ones and to use them in the right way. Federal labeling laws require food companies to specify exactly what their products contain, with an added emphasis if any of the top allergens include wheat, nuts, soy, or dairy. This includes derivatives of the allergens, so that a sauce made with "modified food starch" now must identify its source, such as corn, wheat, or other grains. Many supermarkets are now dedicating specific aisles to wheat- and gluten-free products, with expanded cereal, pasta, soup, snack, and frozen food options. Some stores are voluntarily labeling gluten-free foods at their deli counters and take-out sections as well. A word of thanks to your store manager, with the promise of future purchases, will help maintain and increase this exciting new product growth and attention to labeling.

Several of the recipes in this book specifically call for the use of a certain brand of ingredient. This occurs only when that brand is needed to yield best-tasting and highest-quality results. This is especially true for some baked goods, pasta dishes, and tortilla dishes.

Two companies that I highly recommend for their gluten-free flours are Bob's Red Mill and Authentic Foods. Their preblended flours help save time in the kitchen and result in superb baked goods. Following is a list of other products that I reference within the recipes, all of which I believe you will find both helpful and delicious.

Anheuser-Busch Red Bridge Beer
Authentic Foods GF Flours
Authentic Foods GF Multiblend Flour Mix
Bard's Tale Beer
Bob's Red Mill GF Chocolate Cake Mix
Bob's Red Mill GF Flours
Bob's Red Mill Gluten-Free Oatmeal
Cream Hill Estates Gluten-Free Oatmeal
EnviroKidz Amazon Frosted Flakes
EnviroKidz Vanilla Animal Cookies
Food for Life Brown Rice Tortillas
Food for Life China Black Rice Bread
General Mills Rice Chex Cereal
Gifts of Nature Gluten-Free Oatmeal
Gillian's Bread Crumbs
Gluten-Free Oats Gluten-Free Oatmeal
Glutino Corn Bread
Glutino Crackers
Glutino Honey Nut Cereal
Kinnikinnick Italian White Tapioca Rice Bread
La Choy Soy Sauce
Mi-Del GF Arrowroot Cookies
Mi-Del GF Ginger Snaps
Nature's Path Corn Flakes
Tamari Wheat-Free Soy Sauce
Tinkyada Brown Rice Pastas

CHAPTER 2

SOUPS
CHOWDERS
CHILIS
BISQUES

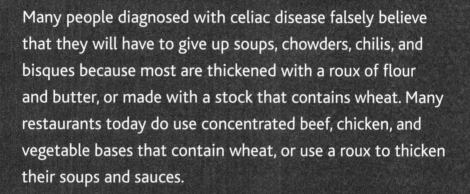

Many people diagnosed with celiac disease falsely believe that they will have to give up soups, chowders, chilis, and bisques because most are thickened with a roux of flour and butter, or made with a stock that contains wheat. Many restaurants today do use concentrated beef, chicken, and vegetable bases that contain wheat, or use a roux to thicken their soups and sauces.

However, this does not mean that a creamy clam chowder, rich French onion soup with melted cheese, or a scrumptious gravy is off limits. A number of gluten-free stocks are available at most local grocery stores. There are also other workable alternatives to thickening soups, as well. Cornstarch, arrowroot, and tapioca starch all have double the thickening power of standard wheat flour. In addition, they are tasteless, meaning that they will not change or overpower the desired flavor of a soup or sauce. It is important, however, to not overcook these agents, as their thickening power will break down when overheated causing the soup to become too thin. When these flours are used correctly, they can help create soups and sauces thickened to perfection and absolutely delicious.

THICKENING AGENTS AND TRICKS OF THE TRADE

Thickening Agents

Following is a list of ingredients that can be used to thicken soups and sauces, but other natural thickeners can also be used for the same purpose. You can use cooked beans to thicken soups and chowders by pureeing them with a little hot stock and returning this mixture to the pot. Other natural thickeners include such starchy foods as potatoes, potato flakes, and rice. For bisques or chowders, puree some of the cooked rice or potatoes with hot stock in a blender, then return the mixture to the soup. This method also works well with vegetables such as carrots or tomatoes.

Arrowroot: Arrowroot resembles cornstarch, and the thickening procedure is the same, but it should be done at a lower temperature. Arrowroot is the better choice when thickening any sauce or soup that contains high levels of acidity derived from wine, vinegar, or citrus juice. Arrowroot-thickened soups or sauces also freeze and defrost better than cornstarch.

Whisk 2 tablespoons arrowroot with 1 cup cold liquid and add to dish just before serving. Simmer; do not boil.

Bean flour: Beans can be used in the same manner as potatoes or rice. Puree beans together with hot stock and add it back into the main ingredients to naturally thicken a soup or chowder.

If using bean flours, whisk 3 tablespoons bean flour with 1 cup cold liquid before adding to the dish. Bring to a boil and allow to thicken to the desired consistency before serving. For more on specific types of bean flours (garbanzo, black bean, and white bean, see pages 18–22).

Butter: Whisking cold butter into a sauce toward the end of cooking will thicken the sauce slightly.

Eggs: Eggs beaten with a small amount of hot stock and cooked in a hot liquid will thicken the mixture. Beating the eggs with a small amount of cream before adding them to the hot mixture will prevent them from curdling.

Cream, milk, and cheese: Whole milk or cream added to soups or sauces and then cooked to reduce the mixture will act as a thickener. Mixing cream with a melted cheese such as Parmesan or Cheddar will result in a thick, smooth sauce.

Cornstarch: This is a white powder milled from corn. When mixed with a cold liquid (e.g., water, milk, or stock) and stirred into a hot soup or sauce, it acts as a thickener. Cornstarch can also be used in pie fillings and custards. Dishes thickened with cornstarch have a glossy smoothness and a clearer appearance than those thickened with flour. I use cornstarch to thicken many of my desserts such as Blaspberry Pie (page 97), Candied Banana Cream Pie (page 104), and No-Bake Rice Pudding (page 165).

Whisk 2 tablespoons cornstarch with 1 cup cold liquid before adding to the dish. Bring to a boil and allow to thicken to desired consistency before serving. Boiling too long will diminish the thickening power.

Gelatin: A protein, which when combined correctly with a liquid, thickens as it cools. Use in pie fillings or custards.

In a small mixing bowl, sprinkle 1/4 ounce gelatin over 2 tablespoons cold liquid. Set aside while the gelatin expands and softens, about 5 minutes. Add 1/2 cup boiling liquid (water or juice) and stir until the gelatin dissolves completely. Blend into your desired filling and refrigerate.

Guar gum: Ground from an East Indian seed belonging to the legume family, this sticky white substance can be used as a thickener or binder. Guar gum is used in many gluten-free commercial foods.

Gumbo filé: A seasoning made from ground dried sassafras leaves, used to thicken gumbos.

Rice flours: Brown, white, and sweet rice flours can be used to thicken soups, but will leave a grainy texture and a cloudy appearance. I have found that rice flours are a wonderful thickening agent for gravies such as turkey, beef, or mushroom. When used in a gravy, rice flour dissolves easily, and will not result in the lumpiness that is common with a wheat flour roux.

Whisk 2 tablespoons rice flour with 1 cup cold liquid before adding to the dish. Bring to a boil and allow to thicken to desired consistency before serving.

Tapioca flour: A starch derived from the root of the cassava plant. Tapioca flour can be used much like cornstarch for thickening soups, sauces, and pie fillings.

Whisk 3 tablespoons tapioca flour with 1 cup cold liquid and add to the dish just before serving.

Yogurt and sour cream: Both of these dairy products can be used to thicken liquid, but they must be whisked into any hot liquid at the end of the cooking process, or they will curdle.

Xanthan gum: Used as a thickener or binding agent for gluten-free baked goods (see page 22).

Tricks of the Trade

Reduction: Involves simmering a liquid over heat, which causes the water to evaporate, leaving the remaining liquid to naturally thicken.

Slurry: A starch (e.g., cornstarch, arrowroot, rice flours, tapioca flour, and potato starch) mixed with a cold liquid, blended into a hot liquid, and brought to a boil until the liquid reaches its desired thickness. When using arrowroot slurry, bring the liquid to a boil, remove it from the heat, and then blend the slurry into the hot liquid.

GLUTEN-FREE STOCKS AND BROTHS

Stock bases, frozen stocks, and canned and packaged broths are now widely available in grocery stores and supermarkets. With the advent of new labeling laws, gluten-free varieties of ready-made stocks and broths are also easier to find. Following is a list of ready-made gluten-free stocks and broths that will save you much time in the kitchen. Always check the labels before use, as companies may add or change ingredients over time in an effort to improve or update their products.

Swanson (www.swansonbroth.com)
Lower Sodium Beef Broth
RTS Beef Broth
RTS Chicken Broth
Natural Goodness Chicken Broth
Vegetable Broth
Organic Broths

Pacific Natural Foods (www.pacificfoods.com)
Organic Low Sodium Chicken
Natural Free Range Chicken Broth
Organic Free Range Chicken Broth
Beef Broth
Organic Beef Broth
Organic Vegetable Broth
Organic Low Sodium Vegetable Broth
Organic Mushroom Broth

Health Valley (www.healthvalley.com)
Fat Free No Salt Added Beef Broth
Fat Free Chicken Broth
No Salt Added Chicken Broth
Fat Free Beef Flavored Broth
Fat Free Vegetable Broth

Imagine (www.imaginefoods.com)
Organic Beef Cooking Stock
Organic Beef Broth
Organic Chicken Cooking Stock
Organic Low Sodium Free Range Chicken Broth
Organic No-Chicken Broth
Organic Free Range Chicken Broth
Organic Vegetable Cooking Stock
Organic Low Sodium Vegetable Broth
Organic Vegetable Broth

Herb-Ox (www.hormel.com)
Beef Bouillon
Chicken Bouillon
Garlic Chicken Bouillon
Vegetable Bouillon

Kitchen Basics (www.kitchenbasics.net)

Beef Stock

Chicken Stock

Vegetable Stock

Seafood Stock

Turkey Stock

Ham Stock

Clam Stock

Pork Stock

Wolfgang Puck (www.wolfgangpucksoup.com)

All Natural Roasted Chicken Stock

Organic Chicken Broth

Organic Beef Broth

Organic Vegetable Broth

Commercial bases, stocks, and broths

Custom Culinary, Inc.
(www.customculinary.com)

Gold Label Low Sodium Chicken Base, No MSG Added

Gold Label Chicken Base

Gold Label Low Sodium Beef Base, No MSG Added

Gold Label Low Sodium Vegetable Base, No MSG
   Added, Vegan

Gold Label Savory Roasted TM Vegetable Base,
   No MSG Added, Vegan

Gold Label Roasted Garlic Base, No MSG Added, Vegan

Gold Label Mirepoix Base, No MSG Added, Vegan

Gold Label Lobster Base, No MG Added

Gold Label Ham Base, No MSG Added

Gold Label Southwest Base, No MSG Added

Gold Label Fish Base, No MSG Added

Gold Label Shrimp Base, No MSG Added

Gold Label Bacon, No MSG Added

Gold Label Zesty Vegetable Base, No MSG Added

Minor's Signature (www.soupbase.com)

Garlic Base-Sautéed

Ranchero Flavor Concentrate

Roasted Garlic Flavor Concentrate

Roasted Mirepoix Flavor Concentrate

Roasted Onion Flavor Concentrate

Roasted Red Pepper Flavor Concentrate

Sautéed Vegetable Base (Mirepoix)

Veal Base

ROASTED TOMATO AND WHITE BEAN SOUP
SERVES 4 TO 6

Ripe plum tomatoes roasted with garlic cloves and drizzled with extra-virgin olive oil give this soup a sweet, mellow undertone. Sweet onions, chicken stock, cannellini beans and fragrant herbs such as rosemary and basil add their unique and enticing flavors.

3 pounds plum tomatoes, halved lengthwise
  and seeded
1/2 cup plus 3 tablespoons olive oil
4 cloves garlic, sliced
Salt and freshly ground black pepper
4 cups chicken stock or broth

1/2 cup chopped yellow sweet onion
1 tablespoon minced fresh rosemary
2 (15 1/2-ounce) cans cannellini beans, undrained
2 tablespoons chopped fresh basil, or 2 teaspoons dried

Preheat the oven to 400°F. Place the tomatoes, cut side up, on a baking sheet and drizzle with the 1/2 cup olive oil. Sprinkle with the garlic, salt, and pepper. Roast until the tomatoes are brown on the edges and tender, 50 to 60 minutes. Remove from the oven and let cool slightly.

Transfer half of the tomatoes to a food processor with 2 cups of the stock and pulse until smooth. Pour into a bowl and set aside. Repeat with the remaining tomatoes and stock.

In a large saucepan, heat the 3 tablespoons olive oil over medium heat. Add the onion and rosemary and cook until the onion is translucent, about 3 minutes. Add the pureed tomatoes to the pot along with the cannellini beans and bring the soup to a boil. Decrease the heat to medium-low and simmer, uncovered, for 20 minutes. Stir in the basil and season to taste with salt and pepper.

Variations:

For a creamier soup, stir in 1/2 cup light cream, half-and-half, or milk when adding the tomatoes and beans.

For a thicker soup, puree 1 can of the cannellini beans with the tomatoes and chicken stock.

AFRICAN PEANUT SOUP
SERVES 4 TO 6

Tommy, a co-worker of mine, asked me to sample a bowl of his famous African peanut soup. After just one bite, I knew that this soup was "one for the book." The recipe was originally written using wheat flour as the thickener. With a few adjustments and the addition of arrowroot, I was able to prepare this delicious soup for all to enjoy.

3 tablespoons peanut oil
1 1/2 cups chopped yellow onion
1 cup peeled, diced carrot
1/2 cup chopped celery
1 cup diced green or red bell pepper
4 cups chicken stock or broth
1/2 cup chunky natural peanut butter

4 plum tomatoes, chopped
2 cups diced cooked chicken
1 1/4 cups milk
Pinch of cayenne pepper
1/2 tablespoon arrowroot
Salt and freshly ground black pepper

In a large saucepan, heat the peanut oil over medium heat. Add the onion, carrot, celery, and bell pepper and sauté until tender, about 5 minutes. Add the stock and peanut butter and simmer for 15 minutes. Add the tomatoes, chicken, 1 cup of the milk, and the cayenne pepper. Simmer for 15 minutes.

In a small bowl, stir the remaining 1/4 cup milk and the arrowroot together until smooth. Add to the simmering soup and stir for 1 to 2 minutes until the soup thickens. Season to taste with salt and pepper.

ITALIAN SAUSAGE SOUP
SERVES 6 TO 8

The hot and sweet sausage combination in this soup gives each spoonful a bit of heat. For those who prefer a little less kick, omit the hot sausage and use 1 pound of sweet sausage.

1/2 pound brown rice pasta elbows or shells
8 ounces hot Italian sausage, removed from casings
8 ounces sweet Italian sausage, removed from casings
1 cup chopped yellow onion
1 cup chopped celery
3 cloves garlic, minced
3 cups beef stock or broth
3 cups chicken stock or broth

1 (14 1/2-ounce) can crushed tomatoes
2 cups diced zucchini
1 cup thinly sliced carrots
1 (15 1/2-ounce) can cannellini beans, undrained
6 ounces baby spinach
Salt and freshly ground black pepper
Grated Parmesan cheese, for sprinkling

In a large pot of salted boiling water, cook the pasta until al dente according to the package directions. Drain and set aside.

In a large pot, combine the sausages, onion, celery, and garlic. Sauté until the vegetables are tender and the sausage is cooked through, about 10 minutes. Stir in the stocks, tomatoes, zucchini, and carrots. Bring to a boil, decrease the heat to a simmer, and cook for 15 minutes.

Stir in the beans, spinach, and pasta. Cover and simmer for 15 more minutes. Remove from the heat, season with salt and pepper to taste, and let rest for 10 minutes before serving. Serve sprinkled with Parmesan cheese.

MUSHROOM SOUP WITH WILD RICE
SERVES 4 TO 6

Blending a mixture of mushrooms with chewy wild rice yields a soup with a sweet and earthy flavor.

2 cups chicken stock or broth
1/2 cup uncooked wild rice
4 tablespoons butter
12 ounces assorted mushrooms, such as cremini, white, and oyster, sliced
1 cup chopped yellow onion
1/2 cup diced celery
3/4 tablespoon minced fresh rosemary, or
   1 teaspoon dried

3/4 tablespoon minced fresh thyme, or
   1 teaspoon dried
2 cloves garlic, minced
8 ounces russet potatoes, peeled and diced
2 cups beef stock or broth
3/4 cup whole milk
1/2 cup dry sherry
Salt and freshly ground black pepper

In a medium saucepan, combine the stock and rice. Cover and bring to a boil over high heat; decrease the heat to a simmer and cook for 30 to 40 minutes, or until almost all the liquid is absorbed and the rice is tender. Remove from heat and set aside.

In a large saucepan, melt 3 tablespoons of the butter over medium-high heat and sauté the mushrooms until golden brown, about 5 minutes. Transfer the mushrooms to a bowl and set aside.

In the same pan, melt the remaining 1 tablespoon butter and sauté the onion, celery, rosemary, and thyme until the onion is tender, about 5 minutes.

Add the garlic and sauté for 2 more minutes. Stir in the potatoes and stock, cover, and simmer until the potatoes are tender, about 15 minutes.

Transfer the soup to a blender or food processor and puree until smooth. Return the soup to the pot and stir in the milk, sherry, and cooked wild rice. Season generously with salt and pepper, cover, and simmer over medium-low heat for 15 minutes.

CARAMELIZED FRENCH ONION SOUP
SERVES 6 TO 8

Patience is the key ingredient in creating this masterful French onion soup. Allow the onions to caramelize slowly to optimize their rich, sweet flavor. I recommend using Vidalia or Texas Sweet onions.

4 tablespoons unsalted butter
1 tablespoon olive oil
7 medium sweet onions, thinly sliced
1 teaspoon sugar
1 teaspoon salt, plus more for seasoning

8 cups beef stock or broth
2 cups dry white wine
Freshly ground black pepper
1 pound Gruyère cheese

In a large, heavy pot, melt the butter with the olive oil over medium-low heat. Add the onions, cover, and cook for 15 to 20 minutes, stirring occasionally, until the onions have softened.

Increase the heat slightly and sprinkle in the sugar and the 1 teaspoon salt. Continue cooking, stirring occasionally, until the onions are golden brown, about 30 minutes. Add the stock and wine and simmer, uncovered, for 40 minutes. Season to taste with salt and pepper.

Meanwhile, preheat the oven to 425°F. Ladle the soup into individual 10-ounce crocks and sprinkle with a layer of Gruyère cheese. Place the crocks on a baking pan and bake for 10 to 12 minutes, or until the cheese is melted and lightly browned.

CORN, POTATO, AND LEEK CHOWDER
SERVES 6

This classic soup incorporating leeks, corn, potatoes, and cheese provides the perfect warmth for an autumn meal.

5 slices bacon, diced
1 tablespoon unsalted butter
1 cup chopped yellow onion
2 leeks (white and pale green parts only), halved lengthwise, cut into 1/2-inch slices, and washed
1/2 cup chopped green bell pepper
Salt and freshly ground black pepper
2 cloves garlic, minced
4 cups chicken stock or broth

4 large potatoes, peeled and cut into 1/2-inch dice (4 cups)
3 cups frozen corn kernels
1 1/2 cups light cream or half-and-half, heated to 110°F
1/2 teaspoon dried thyme
1/4 teaspoon chipotle chile powder
1 cup shredded sharp Cheddar cheese
2 tablespoons minced fresh flat-leaf parsley

In a large, heavy soup pot, cook the bacon over medium-high heat until crisp. Using a slotted spoon, transfer to paper towels to drain. Pour off the fat from the pot. Add the butter and melt over medium heat. Add the onion, leeks, bell pepper, and a pinch of salt and pepper. Sauté the vegetables until tender, about 5 minutes, and then add the garlic. Sauté for 1 more minute, then add the stock and potatoes. Cover the pot, bring to a boil, and decrease the heat to a simmer. Cook for 10 minutes, or until the potatoes are tender. Add the corn, cream, thyme, and chile powder, and simmer for 2 to 3 minutes.

Ladle 3 cups of the chowder into a blender. Puree until smooth and stir back into the pot. Stir in the cheese until melted. Stir in the bacon and parsley and season to taste with salt and pepper.

Chef's Tip:
After cutting the leeks, soak them in cold water to ensure that they are clean.

HEARTY NEW ENGLAND CLAM CHOWDER
SERVES 4 TO 6

This hearty, buttery soup, thickened naturally with the starch of pureed potatoes, makes for a perfect chowder without the need of a roux.

2 tablespoons unsalted butter
3 slices bacon, chopped
1 large yellow onion, diced
2 stalks celery, diced
3 cups light cream or half-and-half
1 cup bottled clam juice
1 (39-ounce) can minced clams, undrained

1 pound Yukon or Idaho potatoes, peeled and cut into 1/2-inch dice (3 cups)
1 teaspoon dried thyme
1 bay leaf
1/2 cup diced green onions, including tops
Salt and freshly ground black pepper

In medium saucepan, melt the butter over medium heat and sauté the bacon, onion, and celery until the vegetables are tender, about 5 minutes. Add the cream, clam juice, clams and their liquid, potatoes, thyme, and bay leaf. Simmer for 15 to 20 minutes, or until the potatoes are tender.

Remove the bay leaf and then ladle 1 1/2 cups of the chowder into a blender. Puree until smooth and return to the pot. Stir in the green onions and season to taste with salt and pepper.

CHOCOLATE-ESPRESSO CHILI
SERVES 6 TO 8

Bittersweet chocolate, coupled with a kick of espresso, adds depth to a great vegetarian chili.

1/4 cup olive oil
3 medium yellow onions, chopped
2 tablespoons chili powder
2 tablespoons ground cumin
2 tablespoons minced fresh oregano
1 (28-ounce) can crushed tomatoes
2 tablespoons honey
3 cloves garlic, minced

4 (15-ounce) cans black beans, rinsed and drained
1/4 cup brewed espresso or strong coffee
1 cup water
1 1/2 teaspoons salt
1 1/2 teaspoons chipotle chile powder
Pinch of ground cinnamon
1 ounce bittersweet chocolate
2 tablespoons minced fresh cilantro

In a large soup pot, heat the oil over medium-high heat and sauté the onions until tender. Stir in the chili powder, cumin, and oregano and cook for 1 minute. Add the tomatoes, honey, and garlic. Decrease the heat to medium-low, cover, and simmer for 30 minutes.

Add the black beans, espresso, water, salt, chile powder, and cinnamon. Bring to a boil over medium-high heat, decrease the heat to a simmer, and stir in the chocolate and cilantro. Simmer, uncovered, for 30 minutes, stirring occasionally, until thickened.

Chef's Tip:
Make this chili the day before and refrigerate overnight. This allows all of the flavors to meld together nicely. Reheat before serving.

WHITE CHICKEN CHILI
SERVES 6 TO 8

An awesome alternative to typical beef chili, this white chicken chili is creamy, spicy, and cheesy.

1 tablespoon olive oil
1 medium sweet onion, diced
2 cloves garlic, minced
1 green bell pepper, seeded and chopped
1 tablespoon minced jalapeño chile (optional)
1 tablespoon ground cumin
2 (15-ounce) cans navy beans, drained and rinsed
1 (15-ounce) can creamed corn

1 (8-ounce) can diced mild green chiles
2 cups whole milk
1/2 cup chicken stock or broth
2 cups shredded cooked chicken
1 1/2 cups shredded white sharp Cheddar cheese
2 tablespoons minced fresh flat-leaf parsley
Salt and freshly ground black pepper

In a large pot, heat the olive oil over medium-high heat and sauté the onion, garlic, bell pepper, and jalapeño until tender, 4 to 5 minutes. Add the cumin, navy beans, corn, green chiles, milk, stock, and chicken. Bring to a boil, decrease the heat to a simmer, cover, and cook for 10 minutes, stirring occasionally.

Remove from the heat and stir in the cheese and parsley. Season to taste with salt and pepper.

CREAMY SHRIMP BISQUE
SERVES 6

A bisque is a thick soup most commonly made with crustaceans and cream. For a variation, try substituting lobster for the shrimp.

2 tablespoons butter
1 pound medium shrimp, peeled and deveined
3 cloves garlic, minced
2 stalks celery diced
1 small onion, chopped
1 carrot, peeled and diced
1 tablespoon minced fresh tarragon
1 1/2 teaspoons grated lemon zest

1 cup dry white wine
1/2 cup dry sherry
3 cups bottled clam juice
1 cup heavy cream
3 tablespoons uncooked long-grain white rice
2 tablespoons tomato paste
Salt and freshly ground black pepper

In a large soup pot, melt the butter over medium heat. Add the shrimp and garlic and sauté until the shrimp turn pink, about 3 minutes. Using tongs, transfer the shrimp to a bowl and set aside. Add the celery, onion, carrot, tarragon, and lemon zest to the pot and sauté until the vegetables begin to soften, 5 to 6 minutes.

Add the white wine and sherry, bring to a boil, and then decrease the heat to a simmer and cook for 1 to 2 minutes. Stir in the clam juice, cream, rice, and tomato paste. Cover and simmer, stirring occasionally, until the rice is cooked, 15 to 20 minutes.

Working in batches, add the soup to a blender and puree until creamy. Return to the pot and season to taste with salt and pepper.

CHAPTER 3

ENTREES

Most cooks new to the gluten-free diet quickly learn that entrées are the easiest of the courses to tackle. One reason is simply that there are many traditional dishes that are naturally wheat- and gluten- free. The greater challenge is in creating those delicious dishes that are typically dusted or encrusted with wheat flour or bread crumbs. This chapter includes interesting techniques and alternative ingredients to meet these challenges. Some of the featured dishes include Toasted Coconut Shrimp with Peach Marmalade Dipping Sauce, Hazelnut-Encrusted Salmon with Cilantro-Lime Crème, and Coffee-Encrusted Beef Tenderloin, all prepared without the use of wheat flour.

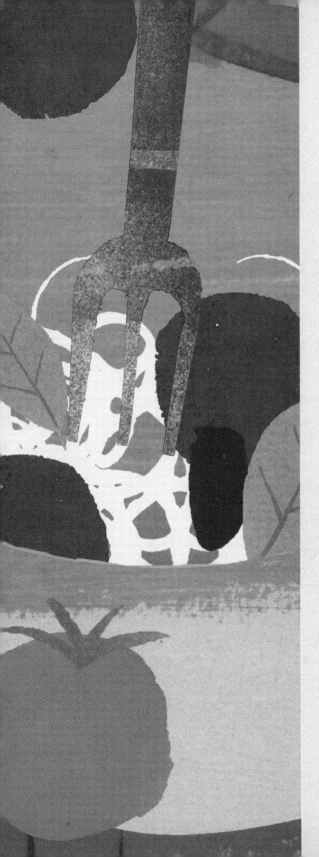

DUSTING AND ENCRUSTING

Dusting or encrusting is the technique of coating beef, pork, poultry, or fish with a combination of herbs, spices, nuts, cheeses, and/or flour mixtures to seal the exterior of a food while enhancing the flavor, texture, and eye appeal of the dish. Encrusting is an opportunity to add extra layers of flavor and texture to a dish. This can be done using a variety of other ingredients in place of wheat or bread crumbs.

Whether you are cooking or baking, the importance of good seasoning, and in some cases even over seasoning, cannot be stressed enough. Dishes served in restaurants often dance on the tongue, simply because they are seasoned throughout the preparation of the dish, not just toward the end. I hope you will enjoy making and eating these dusted and encrusted dishes as much as I enjoyed creating them.

Coconut: Use chopped or grated fresh coconut, or purchase sweetened or unsweetened grated or shredded dried coconut from your local grocery store.

Coffee: Ground coffee mixed with herbs and spices can be a wonderful and unique gluten-free crust for beef, pork, and lamb dishes. For optimal flavor, choose a high-quality freshly fine-ground coffee.

Cornmeal: Cornmeal comes in yellow, white, or blue mixtures, and is another flavorful option for encrusting proteins such as fish and poultry. The Crispy Cornmeal-Encrusted Catfish recipe in this chapter is a scrumptious dish with great flavor and texture. It will leave your guest wondering how it could possibly be gluten free. For more on cornmeal, see page 19.

Gluten-free cornflakes and tortilla chips: Ground in a food processor to the desired consistency, these make a tasty coating for pork, poultry, and fish entrées.

Grating cheeses: Use hard, dry cheeses such as Parmesan or pecorino romano mixed with herbs and gluten-free bread crumbs to encrust any fish or poultry dish.

Herbs and spices: To build layers of flavor in any beef, pork, fish, or poultry dish, simply blend together your favorite herbs and spices, coat the food with olive oil or Dijon mustard, and roll it in the herb mixture before cooking.

Instant potato flakes: Blended with herbs, spices, or cheese, these make an exceptional coating for poultry or fish. Be sure to read the ingredient label, though, as many brands do contain gluten.

Nut meals: Nuts are a wonderful addition not only because of the flavor, but because the natural oils will add moisture to the protein as the nuts are adding an additional crunch.

See the gluten-free flour section (page 23) for variety of nut options.

Pastry crusts: When preparing a crust for a chicken or beef pot pie, or for making a buttery, flaky topping for a seafood stew, follow the recipe for my Cream Cheese Pastry Crust found in chapter 5.

Poppy seeds: These are tiny black seeds that have a slightly nutty aroma and taste. Poppy seeds are excellent for coating breads, cakes, cookies, and muffins, as well as for sprinkling over noodles, vegetables, and fish. Toasting poppy seeds (page 27) will help enhance the flavor and give them a crunchier texture. For more on poppy seeds, see page 25.

Sesame seeds: Sesame seeds have a nutty, sweet flavor that works well with many foods. When the seeds are toasted (page 27), they evoke a flavor similar to peanut butter. They can be used to encrust beef, poultry, pork, and fish, or added to breads or salad dressings to enhance flavor and texture. The Sesame-Encrusted Salmon recipe in this chapter uses both black and white sesame seeds, which not only add superb flavor but also make it a very eye-appealing dish.

QUESADILLAS
SERVES 4 TO 6

A number of gluten-free tortillas are available in the market today. They are typically made from ground corn, teff, hemp, or rice. I prefer Food for Life brown rice tortillas for flavorful, crisp quesadillas.

2 cups shredded Monterey Jack cheese
2 cups shredded sharp Cheddar cheese
1 (10-ounce) can diced green chiles
1/2 cup mild or hot chunky salsa, plus
   more for garnish

1/2 teaspoon Mexican spice blend
1 teaspoon vegetable oil
12 (9-inch) brown rice tortillas
Guacamole and sour cream, for garnish

In a medium bowl, combine the cheeses, chiles, the 1/2 cup salsa, and the Mexican spice blend.

In a large nonstick skillet, heat the oil over medium heat. Add a tortilla to the pan and sprinkle 1/2 to 3/4 cup cheese mixture evenly over the tortilla. Top with a second tortilla. Cook for 1 to 2 minutes, until the cheese is melted and the bottom tortilla is golden brown and crisp. Using a large spatula, flip the tortilla over and cook the other side. Transfer to a cutting board and cut into 6 wedges or triangles. Garnish with guacamole, salsa, and sour cream. Repeat to cook the remaining quesadillas.

Variation:
Try adding broccoli, shredded chicken, spinach, or tomatoes to the cheese filling.

Chef's Tip:
Quesadillas can be kept warm in a 170°F oven until all are prepared.

TOASTED COCONUT SHRIMP WITH PEACH MARMALADE DIPPING SAUCE
MAKES 2 DOZEN SHRIMP

Coconut lovers are in for a real treat—succulent shrimp, deep-fried and dipped in a tangy, sweet sauce. Aloha!

2 dozen medium shrimp, peeled
1/4 cup cornstarch
1/4 cup tapioca flour
1/2 teaspoon Old Bay seasoning
3 large egg whites
1 1/2 cups sweetened finely shredded coconut

Canola oil, for deep-frying

PEACH MARMALADE DIPPING SAUCE
1/2 cup peach marmalade
1/4 cup country Dijon mustard
1/4 cup honey

Pat the shrimp dry with paper towels and set aside. For the coating: In a medium bowl, whisk the cornstarch, tapioca flour, and Old Bay seasoning together. In another bowl, whisk the egg whites until foamy. Put the coconut in a shallow bowl.

Coat the shrimp with the cornstarch mixture and shake off the excess. Dip into the egg whites, and then roll in the coconut. In a large, heavy sauté pan or Dutch oven, heat 3 inches of oil over medium-high heat to 360°F on a deep-frying thermometer. Deep-fry 6 shrimp at a time until lightly browned, 2 to 3 minutes. Transfer to paper towels to drain. Repeat to cook the remaining shrimp.

For the dipping sauce: In small bowl, whisk together the marmalade, mustard, and honey. Serve the shrimp with a bowl of the sauce on the side.

Chef's Tip:
For safety purposes, I strongly recommend using a deep-fat-frying thermometer to maintain the proper oil temperature when cooking the shrimp.

MACARONI AND CHEESE
SERVES 4 TO 6

The pasta for a really good macaroni and cheese must be cooked al dente (tender but firm) before being baked. Gluten-free pastas often require less cooking time than that stated on the packaging. Always steal sample bites of pasta during the cooking process to determine the optimal firmness.

1 pound brown rice elbow or shell pasta

TOPPING
2/3 cup grated Parmesan cheese
1/3 cup gluten-free dried bread crumbs
1 tablespoon olive oil

CHEESE SAUCE
2 cups heavy cream
1 1/2 teaspoons Dijon mustard
3/4 teaspoon kosher salt
1/8 teaspoon cayenne pepper
3 cups shredded sharp yellow or white
  Cheddar cheese

1/4 cup sliced green onions (optional)

Preheat the oven to 375°F and butter a 9 by 13-inch baking dish. In a large pot of salted boiling water, cook the pasta until al dente according to package instructions. Drain and return to the pot.

For the topping: In a small bowl, stir all the ingredients together.

For the cheese sauce: In a medium saucepan, whisk the cream, mustard, salt, and cayenne pepper together. Bring to a boil over medium-high heat. Decrease the heat and whisk in the Cheddar cheese until smooth. Pour the sauce over the pasta, stir in the green onions, and pour into the prepared baking dish. Sprinkle evenly with the topping and bake until the edges are bubbly and the top is golden brown, 20 to 25 minutes.

CRAB CAKES WITH RÉMOULADE SAUCE
SERVES 6

My sister Dana (our family crab cake connoisseur) claims that these are as good as the ones in Maryland. The secret is to use sweet and tender fresh lump crabmeat.

RÉMOULADE SAUCE
1 1/2 cups mayonnaise
1/2 cup Creole mustard
1 tablespoon Worcestershire sauce (see Note)
1 teaspoon hot sauce
1/4 cup finely chopped sweet onions
1/4 cup finely chopped green onions
    (including green parts)
1/4 cup finely chopped celery
3 tablespoons minced fresh flat-leaf parsley
4 cloves garlic, minced
1/2 tablespoon freshly squeezed lemon juice
1 teaspoon capers, chopped
Salt and freshly ground black pepper

CRAB CAKES
3 tablespoons mayonnaise
2 teaspoons Old Bay seasoning
2 teaspoons freshly squeezed lemon juice
2 teaspoons Dijon mustard
1 teaspoon Worcestershire sauce (see Note)
1 large egg, beaten
2 dashes hot sauce
1 pound fresh lump crabmeat, picked over for shell
1 cup gluten-free dried bread crumbs
1/3 cup chopped green onions (including green parts)
2 teaspoons minced fresh flat-leaf parsley
Salt and freshly ground black pepper
Canola oil, for panfrying
Lemon wedges, for garnish

For the rémoulade sauce: In a medium bowl, whisk together all the ingredients except the salt and pepper. Season to taste with salt and pepper. Cover and refrigerate overnight or up to 3 days.

For the crab cakes: In a small bowl, whisk together the mayonnaise, Old Bay seasoning, lemon juice, Dijon mustard, Worcestershire, egg, and hot sauce until smooth; set aside.

In a medium bowl, combine the crabmeat, bread crumbs, green onions, and parsley. Add the mayonnaise mixture and toss lightly until blended. Season

with salt and pepper. Form into twelve 2 1/2-inch-round patties about 1/2 inch thick. Place the crab cakes on a platter and refrigerate for 1 hour.

In a large sauté pan, heat 1/4 inch canola oil over medium-high heat. Add the crab cakes and cook until golden brown, 3 to 4 minutes on each side. Transfer to paper towels to drain. Serve with lemon wedges and rémoulade sauce.

Note:
Lea & Perrins Worcestershire sauce is gluten free.

HAZELNUT-ENCRUSTED SALMON WITH CILANTRO-LIME CRÈME
SERVES 4

A coating of toasted hazelnuts encrusted on a fresh, sweet fillet of salmon adds a buttery, smoky flavor. The cilantro-lime crème adds the perfect bit of tang.

CILANTRO-LIME CRÈME
1/4 cup sour cream
1 tablespoon freshly squeezed lime juice
1 teaspoon minced fresh cilantro
Salt and freshly ground black pepper

1/2 cup tapioca flour
Salt and freshly ground black pepper

1/2 cup hazelnuts, ground
1/3 cup gluten-free dried bread crumbs
2 tablespoons minced fresh rosemary
2 large eggs
Olive oil, for panfrying
4 (6-ounce) salmon fillets, skin and
  pin bones removed

Preheat the oven to 375°F. For the crème: In a small bowl, whisk together the sour cream, lime juice, and cilantro. Season with salt and pepper to taste and refrigerate until needed.

For the salmon: In a shallow bowl, combine the tapioca flour and a pinch each of salt and pepper. Set aside. In a 9-inch pie plate, combine the hazelnuts, bread crumbs, and rosemary; stir to blend. In a small bowl, whisk the eggs until pale and frothy.

In a large ovenproof skillet, heat 1/4 inch olive oil over medium-high heat. Dredge both sides of the salmon fillets in the tapioca flour, then in the eggs, and then in the hazelnut mixture. Place the salmon fillets in the skillet and cook until lightly browned on the bottom, 2 to 3 minutes. Flip the salmon over and repeat on the other side. Transfer the pan to the oven and roast until the salmon is flaky and slightly translucent, 5 to 7 minutes. Serve with a dollop of cilantro-lime crème.

GRANDMA ANNA'S ITALIAN MEATBALLS
MAKES 12 TO 16 MEATBALLS

My most poignant childhood memories center around family visits to my grandmother's home in Brooklyn, New York. Many hours were spent watching her work magic in her kitchen, cooking simple yet amazing Italian dishes that could feed an army. When Grandma passed away, I inherited one of her coveted cookbooks, replete with secret recipes scribbled on torn sheets of paper or folded and tucked away. Her Italian meatball recipe was one of those recipes, calling for a pinch of this, a handful of that, and several shakes of different ingredients. A few minor changes allowed it to be gluten-free, ensuring that many more generations of Landolphis would be able to savor Grandma Anna's famous meatballs.

1 pound ground beef
1 pound ground pork
2 large eggs
1/3 cup milk
1 cup grated Parmesan or pecorino romano cheese
1/2 cup loosely packed fresh flat-leaf parsley leaves, minced

1/4 cup gluten-free dried bread crumbs
1 tablespoon minced garlic
1/4 teaspoon salt
1/4 teaspoon freshly ground black pepper
Olive oil, for panfrying
8 cups tomato sauce

In a large bowl, combine the beef, pork, eggs, milk, Parmesan cheese, parsley, bread crumbs, garlic, salt, and pepper. Working with your hands, mix all the ingredients together until evenly blended.

Moisten your hands with cold water and form the meat mixture into balls slightly bigger than golf balls. Place the meatballs on a platter and refrigerate for 30 minutes.

In a large sauté pan, heat 1/4 inch olive oil over medium-high heat. Add the meatballs and sear until browned on all sides. The meatballs should be cooked in batches so the pan does not become overcrowded. Meanwhile, in a large nonreactive pot, bring the tomato sauce to a simmer. Add the browned meatballs to the tomato sauce and simmer for at least 1 hour.

Chef's Tip:
Serve with your favorite gluten-free pasta.

HONEY SOY-GLAZED CHICKEN WINGS
MAKES 30 CHICKEN WINGS

This recipe makes sweet and sticky chicken wings, perfect for sports-TV snack times, and a *must* on Super Bowl Sunday.

HONEY-SOY GLAZE
1 cup gluten-free soy sauce
1/2 cup distilled white vinegar
2 tablespoons Asian sesame oil
1/4 cup honey
1/4 cup pineapple juice

1/4 cup finely chopped green onions
3 cloves garlic, minced
2 teaspoons ground ginger

30 chicken wings
1 tablespoon sesame seeds, toasted (see page 27)

For the glaze: In a large bowl, whisk together all the ingredients to make a marinade.

Add the chicken to the marinade and toss to coat thoroughly. Cover and refrigerate overnight, occasionally tossing in the liquid.

Preheat the oven to 400°F. Remove the chicken wings from the marinade and place in a baking pan. Pour 1/2 cup of the marinade over the wings and bake for 1 hour, or until the juices run clear after being pierced with a fork, stirring the wings every 20 minutes. Pour the remaining marinade into a small saucepan, bring to a boil, decrease the heat, and simmer for 5 minutes, or until thickened to a glaze.

To serve, place the wings on a platter, sprinkle with the sesame seeds, and serve with a bowl of the glaze as a dipping sauce.

SHRIMP AND VEGETABLE PAD THAI
SERVES 4

The national dish of Thailand, pad thai is one of the most popular dishes in Thai restaurants across the United States. It is also a dream come true for those with gluten intolerance. This authentic version blends succulent shrimp and fresh vegetables in a savory sauce. Tossed with rice stick noodles and garnished with chopped cilantro and a squeeze of fresh lime juice, this dish is at the same time sweet, salty, savory, and sour.

7 ounces uncooked gluten-free rice stick noodles
1/4 cup gluten-free fish sauce
1/4 cup rice wine vinegar
3 tablespoons dark brown sugar
1/4 teaspoon red pepper flakes
1 tablespoon Asian sesame oil
3 tablespoons peanut oil
1 pound medium shrimp, peeled
1 cup mung bean sprouts

2 large carrots, peeled and cut into matchsticks
1/2 cup red bell pepper matchsticks
1 shallot, thinly sliced
2 cloves garlic, minced
1/2 cup unsalted roasted peanuts, chopped
4 green onions, sliced into 1-inch pieces
   (including green parts)
2 tablespoons freshly squeezed lime juice
1/4 cup fresh cilantro leaves, chopped

Prepare the dried rice noodles according to the package directions. You want the noodles limp but still firm. Drain in a colander and set aside.

In small bowl, whisk together the fish sauce, vinegar, brown sugar, and red pepper flakes until the sugar is dissolved.

In a large pan, heat the sesame and peanut oils over medium-high heat. Add the shrimp and sauté until pink, about 3 minutes. Add the bean sprouts, carrots, bell pepper, shallot, garlic, and noodles and sauté for 3 or 4 minutes. Pour the sauce into the pan and, using tongs, toss until combined and coated. When the sauce is almost evaporated from the bottom of the pan, add the peanuts and green onions and cook 1 minute more. Remove from the heat and stir in the lime juice and cilantro.

PARMESAN-PESTO CHICKEN WITH PECANS
SERVES 4 TO 6

A versatile dish, bursting with flavor. Serve it hot for a dinner party or cold at your next cookout. It's a win-win dinner, either way.

12 ounces uncooked brown rice pasta
1 pound boneless skinless chicken breast, cut into
    1/2-inch slices
Salt and freshly ground black pepper
1 tablespoon olive oil
2 cloves garlic, minced
1/4 cup green onions, thinly sliced
    (including green parts)

1/2 cup pecans, chopped
1/2 cup chicken stock or broth
1/2 cup basil pesto (see Chef's Tip)
1 tablespoon minced fresh cilantro
1/2 cup grated Parmesan, plus more for serving
Pinch of red pepper flakes

Cook the pasta according to the package directions. Drain and set aside.

Meanwhile, season the chicken with salt and pepper. In a large sauté pan, heat the olive oil over medium-high heat and sauté the chicken for 4 minutes, or until cooked through. Add the garlic, green onions, and pecans and sauté for 1 minute. Stir in the pasta, stock, and pesto, and toss until the pasta is well coated. Remove from the heat and stir in the cilantro, the 1/2 cup Parmesan, and the red pepper flakes. Serve with extra Parmesan cheese on the side.

Chef's Tip:
Basil pesto can be found in the refrigerator case at your local supermarket.

COFFEE-ENCRUSTED BEEF TENDERLOIN WITH PORT WINE SAUCE
SERVES 4 TO 6

The dry rub of coffee, brown sugar, chili powder, and other spices can be made ahead of time and stored in an airtight container for up to 6 months. It's also excellent on grilled flank steak.

DRY RUB
2 tablespoons finely ground coffee
2 tablespoons light brown sugar
1 tablespoon chili powder
1 tablespoon Spanish paprika
1 teaspoon kosher salt
1/2 teaspoon ground sage
1/2 teaspoon garlic powder
1/8 teaspoon cayenne pepper

2 pounds beef tenderloin, trimmed
1 tablespoon olive oil

PORT WINE SAUCE
1 tablespoon olive oil
2 shallots, thinly sliced
3/4 cup tawny port
1 1/2 cups dry red wine
1 1/2 cups beef stock or broth
5 tablespoons cold unsalted butter,
    cut into small pieces

Preheat the oven to 400°F.

For the dry rub: In a small bowl, combine all the ingredients and stir to blend. Rub the meat generously with the dry rub and set aside.

Pat the meat dry with paper towels. In a large ovenproof sauté pan, heat the olive oil over high heat and sear the beef on all sides, allowing each side to brown before rotating. Transfer the pan to the oven and roast for 25 to 30 minutes, or until an instant-read thermometer inserted in the center of the meat registers 130°F for medium-rare.

While the meat is cooking, make the port wine sauce: In a heavy saucepan, heat the oil over medium heat and sauté the shallots until golden brown, about 3 minutes. Add the port wine and stir to scrape up the browned bits from the bottom of the pan. Add the red wine, increase heat to medium-high, and bring to a boil. Cook to reduce to 1/3 cup, then add the stock and simmer until the sauce begins to thicken. Remove from heat and whisk in the butter.

Remove the meat from oven, tent with foil, and let rest for 10 minutes before slicing. Serve with port wine sauce.

Chef's Tip:
The meat will continue to cook after it is removed from the oven, increasing its internal temperature by 10 to 15 degrees.

Variation:
Add 1/2 cup sliced mushrooms with the shallots in the port wine sauce.

CRISPY CORNMEAL-ENCRUSTED CATFISH WITH BLACK BEAN SALSA
SERVES 6

Fresh farm-raised catfish fillets, panfried and served with a spicy, colorful salsa, make the taste buds dance!

BLACK BEAN–CORN SALSA
1 (15-ounce) can black beans, rinsed and drained
2 cups frozen corn kernels
2 tomatoes, chopped
1 small red onion, chopped
4 green onions, chopped (including green parts)
1/2 cup minced fresh cilantro
1 small serrano or jalapeño chile, minced (optional)
3 tablespoons freshly squeezed lime juice
2 teaspoons balsamic vinegar
1 teaspoon salt
1 teaspoon freshly ground black pepper

3 pounds boneless, skinless catfish fillets
1 large egg
1/2 cup buttermilk
1/4 cup cornstarch
1/4 cup plus 1/3 cup tapioca flour
1/2 cup gluten-free cornmeal
1/2 teaspoon baking soda
1/2 teaspoon baking powder
2 tablespoons Old Bay seasoning
Canola oil, for panfrying
Kosher salt, for seasoning

For the salsa: In a medium bowl, combine the beans, corn, tomatoes, onions, cilantro, chile, lime juice, vinegar, salt, and pepper, and stir to blend. Cover and refrigerate for 3 to 4 hours.

Pat the fillets dry with paper towels and set aside. In small bowl, beat together the egg and buttermilk. In a shallow bowl, mix together the cornstarch, the 1/4 cup tapioca flour, the cornmeal, baking soda, baking powder, and Old Bay seasoning.

In a large sauté pan, heat 1/2 inch of canola oil over medium-high heat. Put the 1/3 cup tapioca flour in a shallow bowl and dredge both sides of the fish in the flour. Dip the floured fish into the egg mixture, and then into the cornmeal mixture.

Panfry the fish until golden brown, about 2 minutes on each side. Lightly sprinkle the fish with salt, and serve topped with the salsa.

CHICKEN ENCHILADA CASSEROLE
SERVES 6

This dish is also called Mexican lasagne, because it consists of tortillas layered with salsa, chicken, and a spicy sour cream–cheese filling.

1 1/2 cups sour cream
1 (8-ounce) can diced green chiles
4 large green onions, chopped (including green parts)
1/2 cup minced fresh cilantro
1 1/2 teaspoons ground cumin

2 cups diced cooked chicken
2 cups firmly packed shredded sharp Cheddar cheese
Salt and freshly ground black pepper
1 (16-ounce) jar medium-hot salsa
6 brown rice tortillas, cut in half

Preheat the oven to 350°F and grease a 9 by 13-inch glass baking dish.

In a large bowl, combine the sour cream, chiles, green onions, cilantro, cumin, chicken, and 1/2 cup of the Cheddar. Season to taste with salt and pepper.

Spread 1/4 cup of the salsa on the bottom of the prepared dish and lay 4 tortilla halves in the dish to cover the bottom. Spread half the filling and 1/2 cup of the cheese on top of the tortillas. Layer 4 more tortilla halves on top of the cheese, then spread with 1/4 cup of the salsa. Spread the remaining filling on top of the salsa, followed by the remaining tortillas. Top with the remaining salsa and cheese.

Cover with greased aluminum foil and bake until heated through, about 40 minutes. Remove the foil and bake an additional 10 minutes, or until the cheese on top has melted. Let rest for 15 minutes before cutting and serving.

Variation:

Corn tortillas can be substituted for the brown rice tortillas.

MAPLE-GLAZED PORK TENDERLOIN
SERVES 4

This is my wife's favorite dinner party entrée, a scrumptious and tender cut of meat that practically melts in your mouth. Searing the pork over high heat browns the surface of the meat and seals in all of its natural juices.

1 1/2 cups chicken stock or broth
1/4 cup gluten-free soy sauce
1/4 cup packed light brown sugar
3 tablespoons ketchup
3 garlic cloves, minced
2 pork tenderloins (about 2 pounds)
5 tablespoons maple syrup
1/4 cup apple cider vinegar
1 tablespoon Dijon mustard

1 teaspoon kosher salt
1/2 teaspoon freshly ground black pepper
1/2 teaspoon ground dried sage
1 tablespoon unsalted butter
1 tablespoon olive oil
1 tablespoon apple cider vinegar
1 tablespoon maple syrup

In a medium bowl, whisk together the stock, soy sauce, brown sugar, ketchup, and garlic. Pour into a large resealable plastic bag, add the pork, and refrigerate for 4 to 6 hours, tossing occasionally.

Preheat the oven to 375°F. For the glaze: In a small bowl, whisk the syrup, vinegar, and mustard together and set aside.

Remove the tenderloins from the marinade and pat dry with paper towels. Sprinkle with the salt, pepper, and sage. In a large ovenproof sauté pan, melt the butter with oil over medium-high heat. Add the pork and sear until brown on all sides. Transfer the pan to the oven and roast for 15 to 20 minutes, or until an instant-read thermometer inserted in the center of a tenderloin registers 145°F. Transfer the pork to a carving board and tent loosely with aluminum foil.

Using a towel or oven mitt, return the pan to the stove top over medium-high heat and add the 1 tablespoon vinegar, stirring to scrape up the browned bits from the bottom of the pan. Decrease the heat to medium and add the maple syrup glaze, simmering it for 2 to 3 minutes. Meanwhile, cut the pork into 1/2-inch-thick slices and overlap on a platter. Remove the pan from the heat, stir in the 1 tablespoon maple syrup, and pour the sauce over the pork.

CAYENNE-DUSTED CHICKEN NUGGETS
SERVES 4

Glutino crackers blended with Parmesan cheese makes an incredible coating that holds nicely to buttermilk-marinated chicken when fried. Finally, a gluten-free chicken nugget that doesn't fall apart during the cooking process!

1 pound boneless, skinless chicken breasts, cut into
   1 by 2-inch pieces
1 cup buttermilk
1 1/2 cups gluten-free crackers, preferably
   Glutino brand
1/4 cup grated Parmesan cheese
1 teaspoon minced fresh flat-leaf parsley

1/2 teaspoon salt
Pinch of cayenne pepper
Canola oil, for deep-frying

HONEY-MUSTARD DIPPING SAUCE
1/4 cup Dijon mustard
1/4 cup honey

Put the chicken in a resealable plastic bag, add the buttermilk, and refrigerate overnight. In a food processor, combine the crackers, Parmesan cheese, parsley, salt, and cayenne pepper and pulse until finely ground. Transfer the mixture to a large resealable plastic bag.

Remove a few pieces of chicken at a time from its plastic bag and allow the excess buttermilk to drip off. Add the chicken to the bag of cracker crumbs and shake until the chicken is coated evenly. Transfer the coated chicken to a plate and repeat with the remaining chicken.

In a large, heavy sauté pan or Dutch oven, heat 3 inches of oil over medium-high to 360°F on a deep-frying thermometer. Drop a few nuggets at a time into the hot oil, cooking until golden brown, 3 to 4 minutes. Using a slotted spoon, transfer the cooked chicken to paper towels to drain. Repeat with the remaining chicken until all is cooked.

For the dipping sauce: In a small bowl, whisk the mustard and honey together. Place the chicken on a platter and serve with the dipping sauce.

Chef's Tip:
Serve the nuggets with any of your favorite dipping sauces, including barbecue sauce or ketchup.

CHEDDAR AND SOUR CREAM CHICKEN STRIPS
SERVES 4

These baked chicken strips, coated with Cheddar and sour cream potato chips, can be prepared using any of your favorite flavored potato chips. Barbecue or sour cream and onion chips make delicious variations.

1 pound boneless, skinless chicken breasts, cut into
   1 by 3-inch strips
1 cup plus 2 tablespoons buttermilk

1 large egg
2 cups Cheddar and sour cream–flavored
   potato chips

Put the chicken in a large resealable plastic bag with 1 cup of the buttermilk and marinate in the refrigerator overnight.

Preheat the oven to 400°F and grease a baking sheet.

In a food processor, pulverize the potato chips, then place them in a large resealable plastic bag.

In small bowl, whisk together the 2 tablespoons buttermilk and the egg. Take 4 to 5 strips of chicken, allow the excess buttermilk to drip off, dip into the egg mixture, and then add to the plastic bag with the potato chips. Toss to coat thoroughly. Transfer the coated chicken to the prepared pan and repeat with the remaining chicken. Bake for 15 to 20 minutes, or until golden and crisp on the outside and opaque throughout.

LASAGNE LOVER'S DELIGHT
SERVES 6

Tinkyada makes wonderful brown rice lasagna noodles that taste just as delicious as the "real" thing. My Italian father, who grew up on lasagne and spaghetti and meatballs, raved about this dish—he didn't even know that it was actually gluten-free.

2 tablespoons olive oil
8 ounces spicy Italian sausage, removed from casings
8 ounces sweet Italian sausage, removed from casings
8 ounces ground beef
1 cup chopped sweet onion
4 cloves garlic, minced
2 tablespoons dried oregano
1/2 teaspoon red pepper flakes
2 (28-ounce) cans crushed tomatoes with basil
1/2 cup dry red wine

12 uncooked gluten-free brown rice lasagna noodles
1 cup minced fresh basil
1 1/2 (15-ounce) containers ricotta cheese (3 cups)
4 1/2 cups shredded mozzarella cheese
1 3/4 cups grated Parmesan cheese
1 egg
1/2 teaspoon kosher salt
1/4 teaspoon freshly ground black pepper

Preheat the oven to 375°F. For the meat sauce: In a large, heavy soup pot, heat the olive oil over medium-high heat. Add the sweet and spicy sausage, ground beef, onion, garlic, oregano, and red pepper flakes and sauté until the meat is cooked through, about 10 minutes. Add the tomatoes and wine and bring to a boil. Decrease the heat to medium-low and simmer for 20 minutes.

Meanwhile, cook the lasagna sheets according to the package directions. Drain and set aside.

In a medium bowl, combine the basil, ricotta, 1 1/2 cups of the mozzarella, 3/4 cup of the Parmesan cheese, the egg, salt, and pepper. Stir to blend.

Spread 1 1/4 cups sauce on the bottom of a 9 by 13-inch baking dish and arrange 3 lasagna noodles on top of the sauce. Spread 1 1/4 cups meat sauce over the noodles, then spread 1 1/2 cups of the cheese mixture over the sauce. Sprinkle with 3/4 cup mozzarella cheese and 1/4 cup Parmesan cheese.

Repeat, layering the sauce, noodles, cheese mixture, mozzarella, and Parmesan cheese two more times. Top with the 3 remaining noodles and the remaining sauce, mozzarella, and Parmesan. Spray with cooking spray a piece of aluminum foil large enough to cover the pan and cover the dish tightly. Bake for 35 to 40 minutes. Remove the foil and bake for 15 to 20 minutes, or until the cheese is golden brown. Remove from oven and let stand for 15 to 20 minutes before cutting.

RICE WRAPS WITH GINGER-LIME DIPPING SAUCE
MAKES 15 TO 18 WRAPS

Rice paper wrappers and red chile paste can be found in most Asian markets and many supermarkets. These refreshing uncooked rice wraps are meant to be eaten cold or at room temperature.

8 ounces small shrimp, shelled
4 ounces uncooked rice noodles (vermicelli)

1 1/2 cups carrot matchsticks
1 1/2 cups finely shredded napa cabbage
1 1/2 cups cucumber matchsticks
1/2 cup chopped fresh cilantro
1/4 cup loosely packed fresh mint leaves, chopped
20 rice paper wrappers (8 to 9 inches in diameter)

DIPPING SAUCE
1/4 cup gluten-free fish sauce (see Note)
1/4 cup freshly squeezed lime juice
1 tablespoon sugar
1 teaspoon honey
1 teaspoon ground ginger
1/4 teaspoon red chile paste
1 clove garlic, minced
1/4 cup minced fresh cilantro

In a pot of salted boiling water, cook the shrimp until evenly pink, 1 to 2 minutes. Drain and rinse in cold water. Pat dry and refrigerate until needed.

Prepare the rice noodles according to the package directions. Drain and set aside in a large bowl.

Dice the shrimp and add to the bowl with the rice noodles. Stir in the carrots, cabbage, cucumber, cilantro, and mint.

Fill a large bowl with hot water. Dip one rice wrapper at a time into the water; allow the excess water to drip off, and place the wrapper flat on a cutting board. Place 1/2 cup loosely packed filling in center of the wrapper. Fold the bottom of the wrapper over the filling, pressing tightly, and then fold in both sides. Roll the wrapper up tightly, pressing the edge

to seal. Set the finished rolls on a platter and repeat with the remaining wrappers and filling. Let stand for a few minutes to set.

For the dipping sauce: In a small bowl, whisk all the ingredients together.

To serve, cut the wraps in half on the diagonal, place on a platter with the filling facing up, and serve with the dipping sauce.

Chef's Tip:
If you prefer, purchase shelled cooked shrimp at the seafood counter in your local grocery store.

Note:
Be sure to read the ingredients on the fish sauce label; not all fish sauces are gluten free.

SESAME-ENCRUSTED SALMON WITH TROPICAL MINT SALSA
SERVES 4

This dish fuses the crunchy texture of sesame seeds with the beautiful colors of fruit salsa and the refreshing taste of mint—a wonderful adventure for the palate. The recipe also works well with tuna or swordfish.

TROPICAL MINT SALSA
1/2 cup finely diced pineapple
1/4 cup finely diced papaya
1/2 cup finely diced mango
1 1/2 tablespoons minced jalapeño chile
1/4 cup finely chopped red onion
1/2 cup minced fresh mint
1 1/2 tablespoons freshly squeezed lime juice
1/4 cup freshly squeezed orange juice
2 tablespoons brown sugar

SESAME-ENCRUSTED SALMON
1/4 cup black sesame seeds
1/4 cup white sesame seeds
4 (6-ounce) salmon fillets, skin and
   pin bones removed
Olive oil, for panfying

For the salsa: In a medium bowl, stir all the ingredients together and set aside.

In a shallow bowl, stir the black and white sesame seeds together. Pat the salmon dry with paper towels and dredge both sides of the fillets in the sesame seeds.

In a large sauté pan, heat 1/4 inch of olive oil over medium-high heat. Add the fish. Cook until golden brown on the bottom, 3 to 4 minutes. Turn the fillets and repeat on the second side. Serve topped with the salsa.

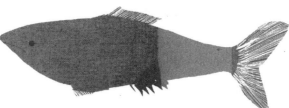

CLASSIC BEEF STROGANOFF
SERVES 6

Adding fresh sage as a last step makes this rich dish incredibly savory.

2 tablespoons Dijon mustard
1 cup light cream or half-and-half
1 cup sour cream
1 1/2 tablespoons olive oil
2 pounds beef tenderloin, cut into 1/4-inch-thick
   strips, 3 inches long by 1 inch wide
1/2 teaspoon kosher salt
1/2 teaspoon freshly ground black pepper

4 tablespoons butter
1/2 cup sliced shallots
1 pound cremini or white mushrooms, sliced
1/4 cup Cognac or dry sherry
1 1/2 cups beef stock or broth
10 ounces uncooked brown rice linguine
   or egg noodles
2 tablespoons minced fresh sage

In a medium bowl, stir the mustard, cream, and sour cream together. In a large sauté pan, heat the oil over medium-high heat. Season the beef with the salt and pepper and add to the pan in a single layer, cooking 3 to 4 minutes until evenly browned on all sides. Using a slotted spoon, transfer the meat to a bowl. Repeat to cook the remaining meat if necessary.

To the same pan, add the butter and melt over medium heat. Add the shallots and cook until tender, about 3 minutes, stirring to scrape up the browned bits from the bottom of the pan. Add the mushrooms and sauté until all the juices released by the mushrooms have evaporated. Add the Cognac, bring to a boil, and stir until the liquid has almost evaporated. Add the stock and cook, stirring occasionally, to reduce to a thick gravy, 15 to 20 minutes.

Meanwhile, cook the pasta according to the package directions, drain, and transfer to a serving bowl.

Whisk the Dijon mustard mixture into the gravy, return the beef, and stir in the sage. Simmer for 3 to 5 minutes, then spoon over the noodles and toss to coat.

CHICKEN PICCATA
SERVES 4

The key to success with this sauce is to use a good-quality dry white wine. My advice for any recipe that calls for wine: If you wouldn't drink it, you shouldn't cook with it.

4 boneless chicken breast halves (1 1/2 pounds)
1/4 cup cornstarch
1 tablespoon tapioca flour
1/4 teaspoon baking soda
1/8 teaspoon salt
1/8 teaspoon freshly ground black pepper
4 tablespoons unsalted butter

3 tablespoons extra-virgin olive oil
1/4 cup dry white wine
3 cloves garlic, minced
1/2 cup chicken stock or broth
3 tablespoons freshly squeezed lemon juice
2 tablespoons capers, drained
1/4 cup minced fresh flat-leaf parsley

Place each chicken breast on a flat surface and cut it in half horizontally. Put each piece between 2 sheets of plastic wrap and pound lightly with a meat mallet or small skillet until the chicken is about 1/4 inch thick.

In a shallow bowl, combine the cornstarch, tapioca flour, baking soda, salt, and pepper. Stir to blend. In a large sauté pan, melt 2 tablespoons of the butter with the olive oil over medium-high heat. Dredge the chicken in the flour mixture and shake off the excess. Add the chicken breasts to the pan and cook until lightly browned, about 3 minutes on each side.

Transfer the chicken to a plate. Pour off the excess fat from the pan and return to medium-high heat. Add the wine and garlic and cook while stirring to scrape up the browned bits from the bottom of the pan. Add the stock, lemon juice, and capers. Bring to a boil, return the chicken to the pan, decrease the heat, and simmer for 2 to 3 minutes.

Transfer the chicken to a platter. Add the remaining 2 tablespoons butter and the parsley to the pan, whisking until incorporated. Pour the sauce over the chicken and serve.

COUNTRY-STYLE CHICKEN POTPIE
SERVES 6

This classic comfort food blends vegetables sautéed in butter with roasted chicken, dry sherry, and cream. Seasoned with a pinch of fresh tarragon, it's topped with a flaky cream cheese crust. It's hard to believe this rich, moist, and delicious dish is really gluten free.

CREAM CHEESE CRUST
1 1/4 cups white rice flour
1 cup tapioca flour
1 tablespoon sugar
1/2 teaspoon baking soda
1/2 teaspoon xanthan gum
1/2 teaspoon salt
1/4 cup shortening
4 tablespoons cold butter, cut into small pieces
1/4 cup cream cheese
3/4 cup milk

FILLING
1 tablespoon butter
1 tablespoon olive oil
1 large yellow onion, chopped
1/2 cup diced celery

3 carrots, peeled and cut into 1/2-inch slices
  (1 1/2 cups)
1 tablespoon minced garlic
2 teaspoons dried tarragon
1/4 teaspoon poultry seasoning
3 cups chicken stock or broth
1/2 cup green peas
1/2 cup corn kernels
1 tomato, seeded and cut into 1/2-inch dice
2 cups diced cooked chicken
1/4 teaspoon salt
1/2 teaspoon freshly ground pepper
1 cup heavy cream
1/4 cup dry sherry
1 teaspoon minced fresh flat-leaf parsley
1 cup diced russet potatoes

For the crust: In a large bowl, whisk together the white rice flour, tapioca flour, sugar, baking soda, xanthan gum, and salt. Using your fingers, a pastry blender, or two dinner knives, rub or cut in the shortening, butter, and cream cheese until the mixture resembles a coarse meal. Stir in the milk. Transfer the dough to a board lightly floured with tapioca flour then, using your hands, form into a dough ball. Wrap the ball in plastic wrap and refrigerate for at least 1 hour or overnight.

Preheat the oven to 350°F and butter a 2-quart casserole dish.

For the filling: In a large, heavy saucepan, melt the butter with the oil over medium-high heat and sauté the onion and celery until the onion is translucent, about 3 minutes. Add the carrots, garlic, tarragon, and poultry seasoning and cook for 2 more minutes. Add the stock and bring to a boil. Decrease the heat to a simmer and cook until the vegetables are tender, about 15 minutes.

COUNTRY-STYLE CHICKEN POTPIE (CONTINUED)

Stir in the peas, corn, tomato, and chicken, then the salt, pepper, cream, sherry, parsley, and potatoes. Simmer for 10 minutes to allow the starch from the potatoes to thicken the mixture.

Meanwhile, roll out the dough between two pieces of waxed paper to a diameter 2 inches larger than your baking dish. Ladle the filling into the prepared dish, then remove the top sheet of waxed paper and flip the crust onto the top of the dish. Trim to a 1-inch overhang and crimp the edges around the rim of dish to seal. Poke several holes in the top of the crust to release steam and bake until the crust is golden brown, 30 to 40 minutes.

CHAPTER 4

SIDE DISHES

Many gluten-free chefs struggle to come up with innovative and creative side dishes to complement the main entrée. This chapter offers some quick and simple side dishes for all occasions, whether you're craving candied sweet potatoes or a bowl of homemade baked beans. These are just a few of the many side dishes that will make your gluten-free meal satisfying and enjoyable.

CRANBERRY-HAZELNUT RICE STUFFING
SERVES 12

This dressing favorite is a blend of brown and wild rices blended with dried cranberries, caramelized onions, hickory-smoked bacon, thyme, and toasted hazelnuts. It's always a must for our Thanksgiving dinner table.

1/2 cup (1 stick) plus 1 tablespoon butter
2 cups sweet yellow onions, chopped
1 clove garlic, minced
7 cups chicken stock or broth
2 cups uncooked wild rice
2 cups uncooked long-grain brown rice
1 tablespoon olive oil
1 1/2 cups thinly sliced sweet onion
2 cups dried cranberries or dried cherries
1/2 cup minced fresh flat-leaf parsley

2 tablespoons minced fresh thyme
1 1/2 cups hazelnuts, toasted, skinned, and coarsely chopped (see page 28)
1 cup chopped green onions (including green parts)
1/2 pound bacon, cooked crispy and crumbled
1/2 teaspoon poultry seasoning
Salt and freshly ground black pepper

In a large pot, melt the 1/2 cup of butter over medium-high heat and sauté the chopped onions and the garlic until translucent, about 5 minutes. Add the stock and bring to a boil. Stir in the wild rice, cover, decrease the heat to medium-low, and simmer for 30 minutes. Stir in the brown rice, cover, and simmer until the rice is tender and most of the liquid is absorbed, 35 to 40 minutes.

Meanwhile, place 1 tablespoon olive oil and 1 tablespoon of butter into a medium-size sauté pan over medium heat. Add the sliced onions and sauté until golden brown, about 40 minutes.

Preheat the oven to 350°F. Remove the pot from the heat and stir in the cranberries, parsley, thyme, hazelnuts, green onions, caramelized onions and garlic, crumbled bacon, and poultry seasoning. Season to taste with generous amounts of salt and pepper, then place in a casserole dish and bake at 165°F for 35 to 40 minutes.

APPLE, SAUSAGE, AND HAZELNUT BREAD STUFFING
SERVES 6 TO 8

The secret to making a good bread stuffing is finding the best gluten-free bread. Two that work very well are Kinnikinnick Italian White Tapioca Rice Bread and Glutino Corn Bread.

6 cups diced gluten-free bread

8 ounces sweet Italian sausage, removed from casings

8 ounces hot Italian sausage, removed from casings

2 tablespoons butter

1 1/2 cups chopped yellow onions

3/4 cup chopped celery

1 1/2 cups peeled, cored, and chopped
  Granny Smith apples

2 parsnips, peeled and diced

1/2 teaspoon dried thyme

1/2 teaspoon dried sage

1/4 cup Cognac or brandy

1/2 cup hazelnuts, toasted, skinned, and
  finely ground (see page 28)

1/4 cup minced fresh flat-leaf parsley

3/4 teaspoon salt

1/4 teaspoon freshly ground black pepper

1/2 cup chicken stock or broth

Preheat the oven to 350°F and butter a 9 by 13-inch baking dish. Spread the bread cubes on a baking sheet and bake until lightly toasted, 20 to 25 minutes. Put in a large bowl and set aside.

In large skillet over medium heat, cook the hot and sweet sausage, breaking the meat into small pieces with a wooden spoon until cooked through, 15 to 20 minutes. Using a slotted spoon, transfer the sausage to the bowl of bread.

Increase the heat to medium-high and melt 1 tablespoon butter. Add the onions and celery and cook until the onions turn golden brown, about 3 minutes. Transfer the onion mixture to the bowl of bread.

Melt the remaining 1 tablespoon butter in the pan and add the apples and parsnips; sauté until the parsnips begin to soften, about 5 minutes. Add the thyme and sage, and continue cooking until the parsnips turn golden brown, 2 minutes. Remove from the heat, add the Cognac, and return to the heat, stirring to scrape up the browned bits from the bottom of the pan until the Cognac is almost completely evaporated. Add the apple mixture to the bread bowl and stir in the hazelnuts, parsley, salt, and pepper. Transfer the dressing to a baking dish and drizzle with stock. Cover with aluminum foil and bake for 20 minutes. Remove the foil and bake another 15 minutes, or until crisp.

SPICED SHRIMP WITH HONEY-MUSTARD DIPPING SAUCE
SERVES 6

This zesty shrimp, an excellent appetizer or party dish, is a unique twist on the standard shrimp cocktail.

Grated zest and juice of 2 limes
2 tablespoons Asian sesame oil
Pinch of red pepper flakes
1 teaspoon kosher salt
2 teaspoons freshly ground black pepper

24 large shrimp, shelled and deveined (tails intact)
12 slices maple- or hickory-flavored bacon, halved crosswise
2 tablespoons minced fresh cilantro
Honey-Mustard Dipping Sauce (page 63)

Preheat the oven to 425°F. In medium bowl, whisk together the lime zest and juice, sesame oil, red pepper flakes, salt, and pepper. Add the shrimp and toss until evenly coated. Cover and refrigerate for 2 hours, stirring occasionally.

On a flat surface, lay out of the bacon slices. Roll each shrimp tightly in a piece of bacon and fasten in place with toothpick. Arrange the shrimp on a baking sheet and bake until the bacon is crisp and the shrimp are pink, 10 to 15 minutes. Arrange the shrimp on a platter, sprinkle with the cilantro, and serve with the dipping sauce.

Spiced Scallops with Honey-Mustard Dipping Sauce:
Sea scallops can be substituted for the shrimp.

ROSEMARY-CHEDDAR POTATO GRATIN
SERVES 6

This dish is a traditional accompaniment to my family's Easter spiral-cut ham. Potatoes layered in a cream sauce with sharp Cheddar and a bit of fresh rosemary—can it get any better than that?

2/3 cup grated Parmesan cheese
1/3 cup gluten-free dried bread crumbs
1 tablespoon butter, melted
1 tablespoon olive oil
1 cup diced onions
2 cloves garlic, minced
1 tablespoon minced fresh rosemary

2 cups heavy cream
2 cups shredded sharp white Cheddar cheese
1/2 cup grated Parmesan cheese
Salt and freshly ground black pepper
6 Yukon Gold potatoes, peeled and sliced
  1/8 inch thick

Preheat the oven to 375°F and butter a
1 1/2-quart casserole dish. For the topping: In a small bowl, stir together the Parmesan, the bread crumbs, and melted butter. Set aside.

In a large saucepan, heat the oil over medium heat and sauté the onions and garlic until translucent, about 3 minutes. Add the rosemary and cook for 1 minute. Stir in the cream and bring to a boil. Remove from the heat and stir in the Cheddar cheese 1 cup at a time until completely melted, then stir in the 1/2 cup Parmesan cheese. Season with salt and pepper to taste.

Place a layer of potatoes in an overlapping pattern in the bottom of the prepared pan and pour one-fourth of the cheese sauce on top. Repeat the process 3 times, finishing with the cheese sauce. Bake, uncovered, until it is lightly brown in spots and bubbly, 50 to 60 minutes. Sprinkle the bread crumb topping over the potatoes and bake for another 15 minutes.

CHUNKY CAPONATA
MAKES 3 CUPS

Caponata is a Sicilian relish made with eggplant, onions, and red bell peppers. For a delicious appetizer, serve caponata on top of a Pecorino Pizza Crust (page 124).

1 (8-ounce) eggplant, peeled and cut
    into 1/2-inch cubes
1/2 teaspoon salt
1/4 cup olive oil
1/2 cup chopped onion
1/4 cup chopped celery
6 cloves garlic, minced
2 tablespoons tomato paste
1/4 cup chopped green olives
1/4 cup chopped black olives

1 tablespoon capers
1/4 cup chopped red or green bell pepper
1/2 teaspoon light brown sugar
1/4 teaspoon freshly ground black pepper
1/4 teaspoon cayenne pepper
1/4 teaspoon dried oregano
1 teaspoon dried basil, or 1 tablespoon fresh, minced
1 tablespoon dry red wine
2 tablespoons pine nuts, toasted (see page 27)

Put the eggplant in a colander and sprinkle with salt. Let drain for 20 minutes, then rinse with cold water and spread on paper towels to dry.

In a large sauté pan, heat the oil over medium-high heat. Add the eggplant and sauté until lightly browned, about 10 minutes. Using a slotted spoon, transfer the eggplant to a bowl.

Place the same pan over medium heat and sauté the onion, celery, and garlic until the onions begin to soften, about 5 minutes. Add the tomato paste and cook for 3 minutes, stirring frequently. Stir in the eggplant, green and black olives, capers, bell pepper, brown sugar, black pepper, cayenne pepper, oregano, and basil. Simmer for 30 minutes, stirring occasionally. Remove from the heat and stir in the red wine and pine nuts. Let cool to room temperature before serving.

ROASTED GARLIC MASHED POTATOES
SERVES 6

These red-skinned potatoes, mashed with slow-roasted garlic, sour cream, and cream cheese, are a family favorite.

3 pounds red-skinned potatoes, cut into 1-inch cubes
1/4 cup roasted garlic cloves (page 28)
1/3 cup sour cream
1/4 cup softened cream cheese or mascarpone,
   at room temperature

1 tablespoon minced fresh flat-leaf parsley
3 tablespoons unsalted butter
1/2 cup heavy cream
Salt and freshly ground black pepper

Put the potatoes in a large saucepan and add cold water to cover. Bring to a boil, decrease the heat to a simmer, and cook until the potatoes are tender, about 20 minutes. Drain and place in a stand mixer with the roasted garlic, sour cream, cream cheese, parsley, and butter. Beat on medium speed until all the ingredients are incorporated. Decrease the speed to low and add cream to the desired consistency. Season to taste with salt and pepper.

Chef's Tip:

These potatoes can be prepared 1 day before serving. Beat 2 eggs into the mashed potato mixture and place in a buttered casserole. Cover and refrigerate until needed. Bake in a preheated 375°F oven for 1 hour, or until bubbly in the center.

JITTER BAKED BEANS
SERVES 6

Each time I make this dish I am reminded of my Aunt Doris and her secret recipe for awesome baked beans. If my taste buds are correct, this one is pretty close. Beans cooked slowly with molasses and brown sugar—no need to say more.

1 pound dried navy beans, rinsed and picked over
1 teaspoon baking soda
2 white onions, diced
3 cloves garlic, minced
1/4 cup olive oil
1 cup strong brewed coffee
1/4 cup packed dark brown sugar

1/2 cup molasses
1/4 cup ketchup
1 teaspoon dry mustard
1 teaspoon salt
1/4 teaspoon chili powder
1/4 teaspoon freshly ground black pepper

In a large pot, soak the beans overnight in water to cover by 2 inches.

Drain the beans and transfer to a large saucepan. Add water to cover and stir in the baking soda. Bring to a boil and cook for 30 minutes. Skim off the foam, drain the bean liquid into another pot or bowl, and reserve for later use.

Place half the onions, half the garlic, and half the beans in the bottom of a slow cooker. Repeat step a second time with the onions, garlic, and beans.

In a medium bowl, whisk together half of the reserved bean liquid and the olive oil, coffee, brown sugar, molasses, ketchup, dry mustard, salt, chili powder, and black pepper. Pour the mixture over the beans, cover, and cook on high for 1 hour. Decrease the heat to low and cook for 8 hours more.

Chef's Tip:

You can also prepare this in a kettle or large pot with a lid instead of a slow cooker. Bake in a preheated 400°F oven for 1 hour, then decrease the heat to 275°F and cook for 5 to 6 hours.

TRI-SPICED ONION RINGS WITH HORSERADISH DIPPING SAUCE
SERVES 6

Any fan of beer-battered onion rings will love this recipe. I always use a hearty gluten-free beer from Bard's Tale Beer called Dragon's Gold.

HORSERADISH DIPPING SAUCE
1/2 cup sour cream
2 tablespoons ketchup
1/2 teaspoon McCormick seasoned salt
1/8 teaspoon cayenne pepper
1 1/2 teaspoons prepared horseradish
1/4 teaspoon paprika

BATTER
1 cup white rice flour
1 tablespoon chili powder
1 tablespoon ground cumin
1 teaspoon cayenne pepper
1 teaspoon salt
2 large egg yolks
3/4 cup gluten-free beer

Canola oil, for deep-frying
2 white onions, cut into 1/2-inch-thick rings
   and separated

For the horseradish sauce: In a small bowl, whisk all the ingredients together and set aside.

For the batter: In a medium bowl, whisk together the white rice flour, chili powder, cumin, cayenne pepper, and salt. Gradually whisk in the egg yolks and beer until a smooth, thick batter forms.

In a large, heavy sauté pan or Dutch oven, heat 3 inches canola oil until it registers 360°F on a deep-frying thermometer. Dip a few onion rings at a time into the batter and then add to the hot oil, cooking until golden brown, 1 to 2 minutes. Using tongs, transfer the cooked onion rings to paper towels to drain. Repeat with the remaining onion rings until all are cooked.

Place the onion rings on a platter and serve with a bowl of the dipping sauce.

SMOKED GOUDA POLENTA
SERVES 4 TO 6

Polenta is a popular dish in Italy and other European countries. Restaurants usually prepare it in two different ways. A firm polenta is baked in the oven, like cornbread, and then grilled; a soft polenta, as in this recipe, is cooked on the stove top.

2 tablespoons olive oil
1 tablespoon minced shallots
2 cloves garlic, minced
4 cups chicken stock or broth

1 cup milk
1 cup yellow gluten-free cornmeal
3/4 cup shredded smoked Gouda cheese
Salt and freshly ground black pepper

In a medium saucepan, heat the oil over medium-high heat and sauté the shallots and garlic for 2 minutes. Add the chicken stock and milk and bring to a boil. Gradually whisk in cornmeal. Decrease the heat to medium and cook for 15 to 20 minutes, whisking frequently until the mixture is thick and creamy. Whisk in the cheese until melted and season to taste with salt and pepper. Serve at once.

Cheddar or Parmesan Polenta:
In place of smoked Gouda, try using 1 cup shredded sharp Cheddar, or 1 cup Parmesan cheese.

CANDIED SWEET POTATOES
SERVES 6

For this topping, I use a gluten-free cereal called Honey'd Corn Flakes made by Nature's Path. It adds the perfect crunch and sweetness.

3 pounds sweet potatoes, peeled and cut into
   1-inch pieces
6 tablespoons unsalted butter, melted
1 large egg
6 tablespoons sugar
1 teaspoon pumpkin pie spice
1/2 teaspoon ground cinnamon
1/2 teaspoon salt

TOPPING
1 1/2 cups gluten-free cornflakes
1/2 cup packed light brown sugar
1/2 cup pecans
6 tablespoons unsalted butter, melted

Preheat the oven to 350°F and butter a 9 by 13-inch baking dish.

Cook the sweet potatoes in a large pot of salted boiling water until tender, 10 to 15 minutes. Drain and transfer to a bowl. Add the butter, egg, sugar, pumpkin pie spice, cinnamon, and salt. Beat with an electric mixer until smooth. Transfer the mixture to the prepared dish and bake for 30 minutes.

While the potatoes are baking, make the topping: Combine all the ingredients in a food processor. Pulse until the mixture is coarse and crumbly.

Remove the potatoes from the oven and sprinkle with the topping. Return to the oven and bake until golden brown, 10 to 15 minutes.

CHINA BLACK RICE CROUTONS
MAKES 2 CUPS

My wife loves Caesar salads, but misses the crunchy croutons typically absent in the gluten-free diet. These garlic, cheese, and herb croutons will make your Caesar salad the hit of the party.

1/2 cup (1 stick) butter, melted
1 teaspoon onion powder
1/2 teaspoon dried basil
1/2 teaspoon dried oregano

4 slices China Black Rice bread, cut into 1-inch cubes (about 2 cups)
1 tablespoon grated Parmesan cheese

Preheat the oven to 350°F. In a large bowl, whisk together the butter, onion powder, basil, and oregano. Add the cubed bread and toss to coat thoroughly. Sprinkle the Parmesan cheese over the bread cubes and toss one more time before placing on a baking sheet and baking for 30 minutes. Remove from the oven and let cool completely. Use now or store in an airtight container for up to 1 week.

Chef's Tip:

Food for Life produces a black rice bread that is made from an exotic strain of natural black rice grown in China. The bread can be found in most supermarkets that sell gluten-free products.

CHAPTER 5

PIES
CAKES

PIECRUST TUTORIAL

Making a piecrust for the first time can be an intimidating experience, even for the well-seasoned chef. However, by knowing a few secrets and following the right directions, anyone can easily become a pastry crust expert.

Right away, most bakers will notice a significant difference in the texture of a gluten-free piecrust compared to that of a wheat-based piecrust. When a wheat-based dough is kneaded into a ball, it naturally becomes stiff as the gluten proteins are activated. On the other hand, gluten-free pie dough is missing that activation, forcing the baker to give up the "kneading" technique and to use more of a "cupping" procedure, similar to that used in forming a snowball.

Here, work the dough just long enough to incorporate the butter and shortening evenly, while packing or forming it into a tightened ball. Next, wrap the dough ball tightly in plastic wrap to help it hold its shape while it is refrigerated. Refrigerating wheat-based piecrusts allows the gluten to "rest." Refrigeration for a gluten-free piecrust also allows the dough to rest, but primarily so that the dough will become easier to roll and form properly in the pie plate.

Sourcing the Ingredients

In making the perfect piecrust, the first things to consider are the ingredients. What exactly is it that makes a piecrust really good? Pie-tasters extraordinaire are always focused on two important factors: Is the crust flaky, and is the crust buttery? Putting all health consciousness aside, there is no way around it—perfect flakiness comes from vegetable shortening, and melt-in-your-mouth flavor comes from real butter. Using a combination of both makes the perfect pastry crust for any pie. The other ingredients needed include a simple blend of white rice flour, tapioca flour, sugar, baking soda, xanthan gum, and salt. Although there is nothing wrong with using a food processor, I still prefer to make my crusts the good, old-fashioned way—by hand. The following are instructions that will assist you when preparing a single or double crust recipe for piecrusts.

Cutting in the Shortening and Butter

After the dry ingredients are mixed together, the next step is to cut in the shortening and butter. This is done to reduce the larger pieces of fat to smaller pieces, while incorporating them into the dry ingredients. These small pieces of butter and shortening are what melt or break down during the baking process, rendering a delicious flavor and proper texture to the crust. It is easily accomplished by using your choice of a standard pastry cutter, two butter knives, or my preferred method—the hands. If using your hands, try squeezing the shortening between your fingers to break the fat down into peanut-size pieces.

Adding the Liquids

At this point, you will add your liquid and incorporate the wet and dry ingredients together until a dough ball forms. Many people use water to bind together a piecrust, but I have found that using milk imparts a richer, smoother flavor that makes a much better-tasting pie. Adding the milk a small amount at a time helps to keep the consistency just right, so that you don't end up with a wet, unworkable dough ball.

A dough ball that is slightly tacky and not too wet is much easier to roll out and shape in the pan. After the ball is formed, wrap it in plastic wrap and refrigerate the dough overnight.

Rolling and Forming the Dough

Start with a clean and clear work area, such as a countertop or a large cutting board that allows you room to roll out the dough. Begin by taking a piece of waxed paper, slightly larger than 12 inches long, and lay it flat on the work surface. Place the refrigerated pastry dough onto the waxed paper and use your hands to press firmly on the dough to flatten it out slightly. Next, take another sheet of waxed paper, lay it flat on top of the pastry dough, and use a rolling pin to roll out the dough. The trick to rolling pastry dough is to begin in the middle of the dough and roll toward the outer edges. Apply just enough pressure on the rolling pin to make the edges the same thickness as the middle. The goal is to roll out the dough, as close as you can, to a 12-inch circle.

Panning the Dough

Transferring a gluten-free pie dough from the cutting board to the pan has always been a challenge for the gluten-free baker. Many have found that the dough cracks and breaks easily, leaving holes and gaps that need to be patched back together. Keep in mind that regular pastry crust dough contains the strong, elastic gluten that assists in holding the dough together and keeps it pliable as it is moved from working surface to pan. When working with gluten-free flours, additional measures must be taken to make the panning process a success.

The key here is to use waxed paper as described, and to have a very heavily greased pan ready for the pastry dough transfer. Begin by removing the waxed paper from the top of the pastry dough. Gently slide one hand under the waxed paper below the dough, supporting it slightly with your fingers. Next, using your other hand, place the opening of the pie pan on top of the dough. Holding your hands as steady as possible, quickly invert the dough into the pan so that the waxed paper ends up on top, with the dough inside the pan.

Place the pan back on your work surface and use your fingers to press the dough into the bottom of the pan. Carefully peel off the waxed paper that is now on top of the dough. There will be an overhang of dough, some of which may break during this step, but can easily be patched later. If you are making a single piecrust, use a paring knife and trim the dough (overhang), leaving a 1-inch overhang of excess dough. Then, using your fingers, begin rolling the excess overhang toward the pie plate rim. Once the entire edge is covered, use your fingers and firmly pinch the dough around the entire pan. If you prefer, you can use a fork to press the tines against the dough, working your way around the edge. Some people prefer to cut this excess dough off, but leaving it on will make a thick, tasty edge around the whole pie.

Prebaking (Blind Baking) a Single Pastry Crust

In the following recipes, several of the pies require a prebaked piecrust. When prebaking a piecrust, some pastry chefs recommend weighting down the dough with pie weights or beans to prevent it from puffing up and cracking. Although this works for some, I prefer a no-weights method. Simply take a paring knife and use the tip to make a couple of pinholes in the bottom of the pastry dough before baking. The holes will bake shut, the dough will puff up ever so slightly, and the bottom will not crack. I find that foregoing the weights in the middle of the pie leaves a lighter, flakier piecrust.

If you do choose the weighting-down method, try using beans instead of weights. Cut a piece of aluminum foil or parchment paper just slightly larger than the center circle of the pie pan. Lay it on the dough and fill it with a single layer of dried beans. This will keep your dough from puffing up and give you a stiffer, denser bottom crust.

Making a Double Piecrust

The recipe for a double piecrust makes enough for two dough balls. The first ball is for the bottom crust and the second is for the top. You will use the same method that you used to roll out the single piecrust, using the waxed paper. The difference is to roll the top crust dough just big enough to cover your filling and to leave a slight overhang on the edge of the pan. You also want to use a pastry brush and a little milk, water, or egg wash to moisten the edges of the bottom crust. This will act as an adhesive when the top crust is attached.

After rolling the dough to the desired size circle, peel the waxed paper off the top of the pastry dough, grip the bottom of the waxed paper closest to you, and flip it over while placing it on top of the filling. Slowly remove the waxed paper from the top of the crust. Next, trim the excess dough from the edges, leaving about a 1/2-inch overhang. Using your fingers, pinch the bottom and top crusts together, working your way around the entire edge of the pie pan. If you prefer using the fork method, trim the dough along the edge of the pan, and then use the tines of the fork to seal the bottom and top crusts together. At this point, use a paring knife to cut 4 to 6 small holes in the top crust, which will allow the steam to escape during baking so the piecrust doesn't crack.

Baking the Pie

Always have a thermometer in your oven to confirm that the desired temperature is being maintained. If the temperature is too high, you will end up with a dark brown outer crust and an uncooked center. If the temperature is too low, you will have a pale, unattractive crust that isn't as flaky as you desired. I recommend baking all pies in the center of the oven, with a large cookie sheet underneath to catch any drippings that may escape. This keeps the oven clean and the kitchen free from filling up with unwanted smoke. Check the pie halfway through the baking process. If it looks like one side is slightly darker than the other, turn or rotate the pie so that it browns evenly. If your pie edges brown too fast, use a piece of aluminum foil to cover the area.

Cooling the Pie

It is very important to allow the pie to cool completely before cutting and serving. This cooling time allows the filling to firm up and the ingredients to reach their desired flavor. If a fruit or custard pie is cut while still hot, the filling will leak out all over the pie plate. Practicing patience during this last step in the pie baking process will make you a much happier pie baker.

FLAKY SINGLE PIECRUST
MAKES ONE 9-INCH PIECRUST

When I began developing this recipe, I set a personal benchmark that it must be as flaky and flavorful as the piecrusts my grandmother made. I have been told by many that this piecrust is the best they've ever tasted.

1 1/4 cups white rice flour
1 cup tapioca flour
1 tablespoon sugar
1/2 teaspoon baking soda
1/2 teaspoon xanthan gum

1/2 teaspoon salt
1/2 cup vegetable shortening
4 tablespoons cold butter
1/2 cup milk

In a medium bowl, whisk together the white rice flour, tapioca flour, sugar, baking soda, xanthan gum, and salt. Add the shortening and butter to the flour mixture. Using your fingertips, a pastry blender, or two dinner knives, rub or cut the shortening and butter into the dry ingredients until they are the texture of a coarse meal with pea-size pieces. Gradually stir in the milk with a fork to moisten the dry ingredients. On a board lightly floured with tapioca flour, form the dough into a ball, then a disk. Wrap in plastic wrap and refrigerate for at least 2 hours or up to 2 days.

Preheat the oven to 350°F. Butter a 9-inch pie plate and set aside.

Roll out the dough between two pieces of waxed paper into a 12-inch round. Remove the waxed paper from the top of the round and invert the pie plate on top of the dough. Place your other hand under the waxed paper and turn the round over so that the dough falls into the pan. Tuck the dough into the pan and then peel off the waxed paper. Let the overhang drape over the edge of the pie plate, while gently fitting the dough into the pan. Using

scissors, trim the dough to a 1-inch overhang. Fold the overhang under evenly. Crimp the edges of the piecrust with your thumb and forefinger or press it with the tines of a fork.

To make a partially baked crust: Using the tines of a fork, evenly poke holes in the bottom and sides of the crust to prevent it from rising when prebaked. Bake 8 minutes before adding the filling and finishing the baking.

To make a fully baked crust: Using the tines of a fork, evenly poke holes in the bottom and sides of the crust to prevent it from rising when prebaked. Bake until golden brown, 18 to 20 minutes. Let cool completely before filling.

Double-Crust Pie Dough:
Double the previous recipe to make 2 disks of dough. Wrap each in plastic wrap and refrigerate for at least 2 hours or up to 2 days. Follow the instructions in individual recipes for rolling out, filling, and sealing the dough.

CREAM CHEESE PASTRY CRUST
MAKES ONE 9-INCH PIECRUST

You no longer have to skip over that broccoli and cheese quiche at Sunday brunch. Prepare this cream cheese pastry crust and add your favorite quiche ingredients before baking. The addition of cream cheese makes this crust slightly softer and more tender than the basic piecrust. It also browns more quickly when baked.

1 1/4 cups white rice flour
1 cup tapioca flour
1 tablespoon sugar
1/2 teaspoon baking soda
1/2 teaspoon xanthan gum

1/2 teaspoon salt
1/4 cup vegetable shortening
4 tablespoons butter
1/4 cup cream cheese
1/2 cup milk

Butter a 9-inch pie plate and set aside. In a medium bowl, combine the white rice flour, tapioca flour, sugar, baking soda, xanthan gum, and salt. Add the shortening, butter, and cream cheese to the flour mixture and use your fingertips, a pastry cutter, or two dinner knives to cut or rub the ingredients into the dry mixture until it becomes coarse and crumbly. Gradually stir in the milk to form a dough ball. On a pastry board dusted with tapioca flour, form the dough into a ball, then a disk. Wrap the dough in plastic wrap and refrigerate for at least 2 hours or up to 2 days.

Roll out the dough between two pieces of waxed paper into a 12-inch round. Remove the waxed paper from the top of the round and invert the pie plate on top of the dough. Place your other hand under the waxed paper and turn the round over so that the dough falls into the pan. Tuck the dough

into the pan and then peel off the waxed paper. Let the overhang drape over the edge of the pie plate, while gently fitting the dough into the pan. Using scissors, trim the dough to a 1-inch overhang. Fold the overhang under evenly. Crimp the edges of the piecrust with your thumb and forefinger or press it with the tines of a fork.

To make a partially baked crust: Using the tines of a fork, evenly poke holes in the bottom and sides of the crust to prevent it from rising when prebaked. Bake 8 minutes before adding the filling and finishing the baking.

To make a fully baked crust: Using the tines of a fork, evenly poke holes in the bottom and sides of the crust to prevent it from rising when prebaked. Bake until golden brown, 18 to 20 minutes. Let cool completely before filling.

CHOCOLATE WAFER CRUMB CRUST
MAKES ONE 9-INCH PIECRUST

I use a chocolate wafer cookie made by Glutino to prepare this piecrust, which is a great choice for a banana cream pie or cheesecake.

30 gluten-free chocolate wafer cookies
2 tablespoons light brown sugar
1 tablespoon chestnut flour

Pinch of salt
4 tablespoons unsalted butter, melted

Lightly butter a 9-inch pie pan.

In a food processor, process the wafers, brown sugar, chestnut flour, and salt until finely ground. Transfer to a large bowl. Add the butter and mix it into the dry ingredients until they are moistened.

If using the crust with a no-bake filling, spread the crumbs evenly in the prepared pie pan, pressing them firmly into the bottom and sides. Refrigerate the crust for 15 minutes. Bake in a preheated 350°F oven for 8 to 10 minutes, or until firm. Let cool completely on a wire rack before filling.

If using the crust with a bakeable filling, fill the unbaked crust and bake according to the recipe directions.

GINGERSNAP PIECRUST

MAKES ONE 9-INCH PIECRUST

Mi-Del Ginger Snaps make a fantastic spicy crust for any type of pumpkin or sweet potato pie.

1 cup gluten-free gingersnap cookies
1/2 cup pecans
3 tablespoons sugar

1/4 teaspoon ground nutmeg
Pinch of salt
4 tablespoons butter, melted

Lightly butter a 9-inch pie plate.

In a food processor, pulse the gingersnaps, pecans, sugar, nutmeg, and salt until finely ground. Add the melted butter and process until the mixture forms moist crumbs. Spread the crumbs evenly over the bottom and sides of the prepared pie plate. Firmly press down on the crumbs to form a tightly packed crust.

If using the crust with a no-bake filling, bake the crust in a preheated 350°F oven for 8 to 10 minutes, or until set. Let cool completely on a wire rack before filling.

If using with a bakeable filling, fill the unbaked crust and bake according to the recipe directions.

VANILLA COOKIE PIECRUST
MAKES ONE 9-INCH PIECRUST

Gluten-free arrowroot cookies made by Mi-Del are perfect for this vanilla cookie piecrust. The flavor and texture of the crust complement most pie fillings.

2 cups arrowroot cookies
3 tablespoons sugar

5 tablespoons butter, melted
1/2 teaspoon vanilla extract

Lightly butter a 9-inch pie plate and set aside.

Put the cookies in a resealable plastic bag and, using the bottom of a small skillet, smash the cookies until finely ground. Or, use a food processor or blender to pulverize the cookies. In a large bowl, combine the cookie crumbs and sugar and stir to blend. Add the butter and vanilla and stir until blended. Spread the crumbs evenly over the bottom and sides of the prepared pie plate. Firmly press down on the crumbs to form a tightly packed crust.

If using the crust with a no-bake filling, bake the crust in a preheated 350°F oven for 8 to 10 minutes, or until firm. Let cool completely on a wire rack before filling.

If using the crust with a bakeable filling, fill the unbaked crust and bake according to the recipe directions.

BLASPBERRY PIE
MAKES ONE 9-INCH PIE

I made this pie for a family cookout in mid-July. My brother-in law, Tony, took one bite and decided he was leaving—with the rest of the pie! Since then, I have had to make two for every party, with an extra pie for Tony to take home each time.

3 cups fresh or thawed frozen blueberries
2 cups fresh or thawed frozen raspberries
1 cup granulated sugar
1 cup water
3 tablespoons cornstarch

1 tablespoon fresh lemon juice
2 tablespoons unsalted butter
1 fully baked Flaky Single Piecrust (page 92)
3/4 cup heavy cream
2 tablespoons confectioners' sugar, sifted

In a blender, puree 1 cup of the blueberries and 1 cup of the raspberries.

In a large saucepan, whisk together the sugar, water, and cornstarch. Add the pureed fruit and cook, stirring constantly, over medium-low heat until thickened, about 20 minutes. Stir in the lemon juice, butter, and the remaining blueberries and raspberries. Remove from the heat and let cool slightly. Pour into the piecrust and refrigerate overnight.

In a deep bowl, whisk the cream and confectioners' sugar together until stiff peaks form. Cut the pie into wedges and serve with a dollop of the whipped cream.

SOUTHERN PECAN PIE
MAKES ONE 9-INCH PIE

This easy pecan pie has a toothsome filling that is chockfull of brown sugar and chopped pecans. It will not disappoint!

2 tablespoons butter, at room temperature
1/2 cup sugar
1/4 cup packed light brown sugar
3 large eggs
3/4 cup light corn syrup

2 cups pecans, coarsely chopped
1 tablespoon vanilla extract
1/4 teaspoon ground cinnamon
1 unbaked Flaky Single Piecrust (page 92)

Preheat the oven to 350°F. Using an electric mixer, cream the butter and sugars together in a medium bowl. Beat in the eggs, then stir in the corn syrup, pecans, vanilla, and cinnamon. Pour into the piecrust and bake for 45 minutes, or until the filling is puffed golden brown. Remove from the oven and let cool completely. Cut into wedges to serve.

KEY LIME PIE
MAKES ONE 9-INCH PIE

This Key lime pie is will leave you puckering up for more.

1 (14-ounce) can sweetened condensed milk
4 large egg yolks
1 teaspoon finely grated lime zest (page 28)
1/2 cup freshly squeezed or bottled Key lime juice

1 unbaked Vanilla Cookie Piecrust (page 96)
1 1/2 cups heavy cream
2 tablespoons sugar

Preheat the oven to 350°F. In a medium bowl, whisk the condensed milk and egg yolks together until blended. Add the lime zest and juice and continue whisking until the mixture slightly thickens.

Pour the filling into the piecrust and bake for 15 minutes, or until firm to touch. Remove from the oven and let cool completely. Cover loosely with plastic wrap and refrigerate overnight.

In a deep bowl, beat the heavy cream until soft peaks form. Add sugar and beat until stiff peaks form. Using a rubber spatula or a frosting spatula, spread the whipped cream evenly over the pie, then lift the spatula to make peaks in the whipped cream. Cut into wedges to serve.

Chef's Tip:

Do not store the pie in the refrigerator for more than 1 day, as the whipped cream will begin to break down.

SUGAR AND SPICE APPLE PIE
MAKES ONE 9-INCH PIE

This American classic delivers a luscious burst of brown sugar and cinnamon. Serve it on its own, or with vanilla ice cream.

3 pounds McIntosh apples (6 to 8), peeled, cored, and thinly sliced
1 1/2 cups packed light brown sugar
2 tablespoons freshly squeezed lemon juice
1 teaspoon ground cinnamon

1/2 teaspoon ground nutmeg
1/4 teaspoon salt
Double-Crust Pie Dough (page 92)
1 tablespoon cornstarch
4 tablespoons unsalted butter, cut into bits

Preheat the oven to 425°F. In a large bowl, combine the apples, brown sugar, lemon juice, cinnamon, nutmeg, and salt. Stir to blend. Let stand for 15 minutes.

Roll out the dough between two pieces of waxed paper into a 12-inch round. Remove the waxed paper from the top of the round and invert the pie plate on top of the dough. Place your other hand under the waxed paper and turn the round over so that the dough falls into the pan. Tuck the dough into the pan and then peel off the waxed paper. Let the overhang drape over the edge of the pie plate, while gently fitting the dough into the pan. Using scissors, trim the dough to a 1-inch overhang. Fold the overhang under evenly. Crimp the edges of the piecrust with your thumb and forefinger or press it with the tines of a fork.

Stir the cornstarch into the filling and pour into the pie shell, smoothing the top with a rubber spatula. Sprinkle the butter over the filling.

Roll the other dough ball into an 12-inch round between two pieces of waxed paper. Remove the waxed paper from the top of the dough round and invert the dough over the filling, carefully peeling off the waxed paper. Using your fingers, tuck the edges of the top crust under the lower crust and press together lightly to form a seal, and using a knife, trim the dough even with the edge of the pan. Then, using a fork, crimp the edges of the piecrust around the border of the pan.

Cut a few air vents in the top crust and bake the pie for 20 minutes. Decrease the oven temperature to 300°F and continue baking for another 20 to 25 minutes, or until golden brown. Remove from the oven and let cool completely on a wire rack. Cut into wedges to serve.

Chef's Tip:
To avoid a mess, place a sheet pan under the pie while baking in the oven, to catch drippings.

BLUEBERRY AND WHIPPED CREAM PIE
MAKES ONE 9-INCH PIE

If fresh blueberries are not in season, frozen blueberries work just as well.

3 tablespoons cornstarch
1/2 cup plus 2 tablespoons water
4 cups fresh or thawed frozen blueberries
1/2 cup sugar
2 teaspoons freshly squeezed lemon juice

Pinch of salt
1 fully baked Flaky Single Piecrust (page 92)
1 cup heavy cream
1 tablespoon sugar

In a small bowl, whisk together the cornstarch and the 2 tablespoons water.

In a heavy, medium saucepan combine 2 cups of the blueberries, the sugar, and the 1/2 cup of the water. Bring to a boil over medium-high heat, stirring to dissolve the sugar, 3 to 4 minutes. Stir in the cornstarch mixture, lemon juice, and salt. Stir constantly until the mixture becomes thick but still pourable, about 1 minute. Remove from the heat and stir in the remaining blueberries. Pour the mixture into the pie shell, let cool for 1 hour, then refrigerate overnight.

In a deep bowl, beat the heavy cream until soft peaks form. Add sugar and beat until stiff peaks form. Using a rubber spatula or a frosting spatula, spread the whipped cream evenly over the pie, then lift the spatula to make peaks in the whipped cream. Cut into wedges to serve.

Chef's Tip:

Do not store the pie in the refrigerator for more than 1 day, as the whipped cream will begin to break down.

CHERRY PIE WITH COCONUT CRUMB TOPPING
MAKES ONE 9-INCH PIE

The coconut-oatmeal blend gives this cherry pie a unique, crunchy topping. It will be an original at any neighborhood cookout!

TOPPING
1/2 cup sweet rice flour
1/2 cup brown rice flour
1/2 cup packed light brown sugar
1/3 cup gluten-free old-fashioned oats (Bob's Red
    Mill, Cream Hill Estates, or Gluten-Free Oats)
1/3 cup sweetened flaked coconut

1/4 teaspoon salt
1/4 teaspoon ground cinnamon
1/2 cup (1 stick) cold unsalted butter, cut into bits

2 (21-ounce) cans cherry pie filling
1 unbaked Flaky Single Piecrust (page 92)

Preheat the oven to 425°F. For the topping: In a small bowl, combine the sweet rice flour, brown rice flour, brown sugar, oats, coconut, salt, and cinnamon. Stir to blend. Add the butter and, using your fingers, a pastry blender, or two dinner knives, rub or cut in the butter until the mixture is the texture of coarse meal. Cover and refrigerate.

Pour the cherry pie filling into the piecrust and evenly spread it with a rubber spatula.

Bake the pie for 15 minutes. Sprinkle the topping evenly on the pie, decrease the heat to 375°F, and bake for 40 to 45 minutes, or until bubbly in the center. If the topping begins to brown too quickly, cover it with aluminum foil.

Remove from the oven and let cool completely. Cut into wedges to serve.

DECADENT CHOCOLATE CREAM PIE
MAKES ONE 9-INCH PIE

Last summer, our friends John and Lisa Duda came to dinner at our home with their ten children. Four of these rich and creamy pies were devoured in a matter of minutes.

2/3 cup granulated sugar
1/4 cup cornstarch
1/2 teaspoon salt
4 large egg yolks
3 cups light cream or half-and-half
5 ounces bittersweet chocolate, melted
2 ounces unsweetened chocolate, melted

2 tablespoons unsalted butter, softened,
   at room temperature
1 teaspoon vanilla extract
1 fully baked Flaky Single Piecrust (page 92)
3/4 cup heavy cream
1 tablespoon confectioners' sugar, sifted

For the filling: In a large, heavy saucepan, whisk together the sugar, cornstarch, salt, and egg yolks. Place over medium heat and gradually whisk in the cream; continue to whisk until the mixture comes to a boil. Decrease the heat to low and simmer for another minute or two, until the mixture thickens. Remove from the heat and whisk in the chocolate, butter, and vanilla. Cover the filling with a buttered round of waxed paper that rests directly on the surface of the filling. Let cool at room temperature for 20 minutes, then place in a refrigerator for 1 to 2 hours.

Pour the filling into the piecrust and spread evenly with a rubber spatula. Loosely cover with plastic wrap and refrigerate for at least 6 hours or overnight.

In a deep bowl, whisk the cream until soft peaks form. Add the confectioners' sugar and beat until stiff peaks form. Using a rubber spatula or frosting spatula, spread the whipped cream evenly over the surface of the pie, then make decorative swirls or peaks.

Chef's Tip:

Do not store the pie in the refrigerator for more than one day, as the whipped cream will begin to break down.

CANDIED BANANA CREAM PIE
MAKES ONE 9-INCH PIE

My wife has always insisted that she doesn't like banana cream pie. After trying this one, topped with chopped peanut butter cups, she changed her mind.

1/2 cup sugar
1/4 cup cornstarch
1/8 teaspoon salt
2 cups light cream or half-and-half
2 large egg yolks
1 1/2 teaspoons pure vanilla extract
2 tablespoons unsalted butter,
  cut into 1/2-inch pieces

1 fully baked Flaky Single Piecrust (page 92)
3 ripe bananas, peeled and cut into 1/4-inch slices
3/4 cup peanut butter cups, finely chopped (about
  8 full-size peanut butter cups)
1 cup heavy cream
1/4 cup confectioners' sugar

In a heavy, medium saucepan, combine the granulated sugar, cornstarch, and salt. Stir to blend. Whisk in the cream and egg yolks. Cook over medium heat, whisking constantly, until the mixture thickens and boils, about 5 minutes. Remove from the heat and whisk in the vanilla and the butter, one piece at a time. Transfer the pastry cream to a large bowl and let cool, whisking occasionally.

Evenly spread one-third of the pastry cream in the piecrust, followed by 1/4 cup of the chopped peanut butter cups and half the bananas. Repeat a second time. Spread the remaining pastry cream over the bananas and sprinkle with 2 tablespoons chopped peanut butter cups.

In a deep bowl, whisk the cream until soft peaks form. Add the confectioners' sugar and whisk until stiff peaks form. Using a rubber spatula, mound the whipped cream on top of the custard and spread out evenly, then form into peaks or swirls. Sprinkle the remaining 2 tablespoons chopped peanut butter cups over whipped cream and refrigerate until serving time.

Chef's Tip:

Do not store the pie in the refrigerator for more than 1 day, as the whipped cream will begin to break down.

CARAMEL NUT PIE
MAKES ONE 9-INCH PIE

Walnuts, pecans, and almonds are folded into creamy caramel, baked in a buttery crust, and drizzled with melted white chocolate. Kiss your diet good-bye!

1 3/4 cups sugar
1/4 cup water
2/3 cup heavy cream
2 tablespoons unsalted butter, cut into pieces
1 tablespoon honey
1 teaspoon vanilla extract

1 cup walnuts, chopped
1/2 cup pecans, chopped
1/2 cup whole almonds, chopped
1 unbaked Flaky Single Piecrust (page 92)
2 ounces white chocolate, chopped
Vanilla ice cream, for serving

Preheat the oven to 375°F. In a heavy, medium saucepan, combine the sugar and water and stir over medium-low heat until the sugar dissolves. Increase the heat to medium and bring the mixture to a boil without stirring. Cook, again without stirring, for about 10 minutes, occasionally swirling the pan, until the mixture turns light brown.

Gradually whisk in the cream (take care, as it will spatter), then stir in the butter, honey, and vanilla. Stir in the nuts and pour the mixture into the piecrust. Bake for 15 to 20 minutes, or until hot and bubbly. Remove from the oven and let cool completely on a wire rack.

In a stainless-steel bowl set over a saucepan with 2 inches of barely simmering water, melt the white chocolate until smooth. Using a fork, drizzle the white chocolate decoratively over the pie. Cut into wedges and serve with vanilla ice cream.

DOUBLE-DOSAGE PIE
MAKES ONE 9-INCH PIE

The best of both worlds in every bite—this delightful combination of smooth and fragrant pumpkin with crunchy, sweet pecans makes for a unique holiday pie.

PUMPKIN FILLING
1 cup canned solid-pack pumpkin
2/3 cup light cream or half-and-half
1/2 cup packed light brown sugar
1 large egg
1 large egg yolk
1/2 teaspoon vanilla extract
1/2 teaspoon ground cinnamon
1/4 teaspoon ground ginger
1/4 teaspoon salt
1/8 teaspoon ground nutmeg

PECAN FILLING
1/2 cup light corn syrup
1/2 cup packed light brown sugar
2 tablespoons unsalted butter, melted
1 large egg
1 large egg yolk
1/2 teaspoon vanilla extract
1/4 teaspoon ground cinnamon
1/8 teaspoon salt
3/4 cup pecans, chopped, plus 3/4 cup pecan halves

1 unbaked Flaky Single Piecrust (page 92)

Preheat the oven to 425°F. For the pumpkin pie filling: In a large bowl, combine all the ingredients and whisk until blended.

In a medium bowl, combine the corn syrup, brown sugar, butter, egg, egg yolk, vanilla, cinnamon, and salt. Stir until blended. Stir in the chopped pecans and pecan halves.

Pour the pumpkin filling into the piecrust and spread it out evenly with a rubber spatula. Pour the pecan filling on top of the pumpkin filling and spread it out evenly again, making sure all the pecan halves are submerged.

Bake the pie for 10 minutes, then decrease the heat to 325°F and bake for 40 to 45 minutes until the edges are puffed and a toothpick inserted in the center comes out clean.

Remove from the oven and let cool completely. Cut into wedges to serve.

WALNUT-GINGER PUMPKIN PIE
MAKES ONE 9-INCH PIE

This pumpkin pie has Thanksgiving dinner written all over it: nutmeg, cinnamon, and clove flavors blended into a gingersnap piecrust.

1 1/2 tablespoon unflavored gelatin
1/2 cup plus 2 tablespoons water
1 1/2 cups canned solid-pack pumpkin
1/2 cup sugar
1/2 teaspoon salt
3/4 teaspoon ground cinnamon

1/4 teaspoon ground ginger
1/8 teaspoon ground nutmeg
1/8 teaspoon ground cloves
1 cup heavy cream
1 prebaked Gingersnap Piecrust (page 95)
1/4 cup chopped walnuts for garnish

In a medium bowl, stir together the unflavored gelatin and the 2 tablespoons water. Set aside to let the gelatin soften, about 5 minutes.

Meanwhile, combine the pumpkin, sugar, salt, cinnamon, ginger, nutmeg, and cloves in a saucepan and stir over medium heat until the sugar dissolves.

In a small saucepan, bring the 1/2 cup water to a boil over high heat and stir into the gelatin. Continue stirring until the gelatin completely dissolves. Add to the pumpkin mixture and stir until blended. Set aside to cool.

In a deep bowl, whisk the heavy cream until soft peaks form.

Using a rubber spatula, carefully fold the whipped cream into the cooled pumpkin mixture and then pour the filling into the piecrust. Cover with plastic wrap, and refrigerate for at least 3 hours or up to 2 days.

To serve, sprinkle the pie with the chopped walnuts and cut it into wedges.

WHITE CHOCOLATE-STRAWBERRY PIE
MAKES ONE 9-INCH PIE

A summertime favorite: fresh, juicy strawberries drizzled with melted white chocolate on top of a sweet cream cheese filling.

2 cups white chocolate chips
1 (8-ounce) package cream cheese,
   at room temperature
5 tablespoons sugar

1 teaspoon vanilla extract
1/3 cup vanilla yogurt
1 prebaked Vanilla Cookie Piecrust (page 96)
4 cups fresh strawberries, hulled and halved

Put 1 1/2 cups of the white chocolate chips in a stainless-steel bowl set over a saucepan with 2 inches of boiling water. When the chips begin to melt, stir until smooth and creamy and set aside.

With an electric mixer, beat the cream cheese until light and fluffy, about 5 minutes. Gradually beat in the sugar, vanilla extract, and melted white chocolate chips until blended. Add the yogurt and beat until completely incorporated. Pour into the piecrust and spread out evenly with a rubber spatula. Cover loosely with aluminum foil and refrigerate overnight.

Starting on the outside of the pie and working inward, place the strawberries, cut side down, in a single layer of circles until the pie is covered.

Melt the remaining 1/2 cup white chocolate chips over barely simmering water until smooth and drizzle over the strawberries. Tent the pie with aluminum foil and refrigerate for up to 1 day. Cut into wedges to serve.

CHOCOLATE CHIP CHEESECAKE
MAKES ONE 9-INCH CHEESECAKE

This cheesecake can also be made with the Chocolate Wafer Crumb Crust (page 94) for an extra hit of chocolate.

3 (8-ounce) packages cream cheese, at room temperature
3/4 cup sugar
3 large eggs
1 teaspoon vanilla extract
1 2/3 cups semisweet chocolate chips

1 unbaked Vanilla Cookie Piecrust (page 96)

TOPPING
1/3 cup semisweet chocolate chips
2 tablespoons heavy cream

Preheat the oven to 450°F. Using an electric mixer, beat together the cream cheese and sugar on medium speed until soft and smooth. Add the eggs and vanilla and continue beating. Using a rubber spatula, fold in the 1 2/3 cups chocolate chips.

Pour the filling into the piecrust and bake for 10 minutes. Decrease the heat to 250°F. Bake for 25 to 30 minutes, or until the filling is set and wiggles slightly. Remove from the oven and let cool completely on a wire rack.

For the topping: Place the 1/3 cup chocolate chips and heavy cream in a microwave-safe bowl. Microwave on high for 30 to 40 seconds until the chips are almost melted. Stir with a rubber spatula until smooth, and spread evenly over the cheesecake.

Refrigerate until the topping has set, about 1 hour. Cut into wedges to serve.

BITTERSWEET CHOCOLATE— WALNUT CAKE
MAKES ONE 9-INCH CAKE

This one-of-a-kind, dark fudgy hybrid of a flourless chocolate cake and a chocolate lava cake is baked just long enough to leave the center moist and gooey. A dollop of whipped cream flavored with orange zest and your choice of Kahlúa, Grand Marnier, or amaretto makes it irresistible.

5 tablespoons unsalted butter
6 ounces bittersweet chocolate, chopped
1/2 cup packed light brown sugar
1/2 cup sugar
1/8 teaspoon salt
2 large eggs
1 teaspoon vanilla extract
1/2 cup walnuts, chopped and toasted (see page 27)

TOPPING
1 cup heavy cream
1 tablespoon sugar
1 teaspoon grated orange zest (page 28)
1 tablespoon Kahlúa, Grand Marnier, or
    amaretto liqueur

8 fresh mint leaves, for garnish

Preheat the oven to 350°F. Line a 9-inch pan with buttered foil so it overlaps the edges.

Put the butter in a microwavable glass bowl with the chocolate. Microwave on high for 1 minute, and then let rest for 2 to 3 minutes. Microwave on high again for 1 minute and then stir until smooth.

In a medium bowl, whisk together the brown sugar, 1/2 cup sugar, salt, eggs, and vanilla until smooth. Stir in the chocolate and walnuts, and then pour the batter into the prepared pan. Bake for 25 to 30 minutes, or until the cake is dry and slightly cracked on the surface. Remove from the oven and let cool completely on a wire rack before lifting the cake from the pan and setting it on a cutting board.

For the topping: Using an electric mixer, beat the cream, 1 tablespoon sugar, orange zest, and Kahlúa until stiff peaks form. Cut the cake into slices and serve with a dollop of topping, garnished with a mint leaf.

RICOTTA CAKE WITH FRESH BERRIES
MAKES ONE 10-INCH CAKE

This ricotta cake is lighter and less dense than your usual cheesecake. Serve with fresh berries on top and a sprinkle of confectioners' sugar for a delicious summertime dessert.

CRUST
1 (8-ounce) bag gluten-free Mi-Del Arrowroot Cookies
3 tablespoons sugar
4 tablespoons butter, melted

1 (15-ounce) container ricotta cheese
1/2 cup sour cream
4 ounces cream cheese, at room temperature
1 large egg
2 large egg whites

3/4 cup sugar
1/4 cup white rice flour
1 teaspoon xanthan gum
1 teaspoon vanilla extract
1 teaspoon grated lemon zest
1/4 teaspoon salt
1 cup fresh strawberries, hulled and sliced
3/4 cup fresh raspberries
3/4 cup fresh blueberries
Confectioners' sugar, for dusting

Preheat the oven to 325°F. Butter a 10-inch springform pan.

For the crust: In a food processor, combine the cookies and the 3 tablespoons sugar and process into crumbs. Pour into a medium bowl and stir in the melted butter. Spread the crumbs evenly and firmly over the bottom and sides of the prepared pan. Bake for 8 minutes, or until golden and crisp. Remove from the oven and let cool completely on a wire rack.

In a food processor, process the ricotta cheese on high speed until smooth and creamy. Add the sour cream, cream cheese, egg, egg whites, 3/4 cup sugar, rice flour, xanthan gum, vanilla, lemon zest, and salt. Process until blended, then pour into the prepared crust and bake until the center is set, 45 to 50 minutes.

Remove from the oven and let cool on wire rack. Cover and refrigerate for at least 4 hours or up to 2 days. Layer the top of the cake with the berries and dust with confectioners' sugar. Cut into wedges to serve.

LEMONY ALMOND CAKE
MAKES ONE 9-INCH CAKE

No lemon juice in this recipe, only the pungent and tangy flavor of lemon zest. A very refreshing dessert.

1 1/3 cups slivered almonds
8 tablespoons granulated sugar
4 large eggs, separated
5 teaspoons grated lemon zest

1/2 teaspoon ground cinnamon
Pinch of salt
Confectioners' sugar, for dusting
Fresh berries and whipped cream, for garnish

Preheat the oven to 375°F. Butter a 9-inch cake pan. Line the bottom with a round of waxed paper and butter the paper.

In a food processor, process the almonds with 2 tablespoons of the sugar, until finely ground. Transfer to a medium bowl and set aside.

In the food processor, process the egg yolks, 2 tablespoons of the sugar, the lemon zest, cinnamon, and salt together for 1 minute. Add to the almond mixture and stir until blended. Set aside.

Using an electric mixer, beat the egg whites on low speed until foamy, then increase to medium speed and beat until soft peaks form. Gradually beat in the remaining 4 tablespoons sugar and continue beating until stiff, glossy peaks form. Fold the egg whites into the almond mixture, pour into the prepared pan, and smooth the top. Bake for 30 to 35 minutes, or until a toothpick inserted in the center comes out clean.

Remove from the oven and let cool completely on a wire rack. Unmold onto a plate and remove the paper. Dust with confectioners' sugar. Cut into wedges and serve with fresh berries and a dollop of whipped cream.

WHOOPIE PIES
MAKES 12 INDIVIDUAL PIES

Whoopie pies are chocolate cake sandwiches filled with a sugary white frosting. These were a best seller when I owned a bakery near the University of Connecticut. To save time, use the chocolate cake mix from Bob's Red Mill and follow this recipe.

1/2 cup (1 stick) butter at room temperature
1 (16-ounce) package Bob's Red Mill gluten-free
   chocolate cake mix
3/4 cup milk
1 tablespoon freshly squeezed lemon juice
2 large eggs
1/3 cup warm water (110°F)

2 teaspoons vanilla extract
1/4 cup shortening
3 1/4 cups confectioners' sugar, sifted
1/4 cup milk
1/2 teaspoon vanilla extract
Confectioners' sugar, for dusting

Preheat the oven to 350°F. Butter two baking sheets.

Using an electric mixer, cream the butter on medium speed until smooth. Decrease the speed to low and gradually add the cake mix, the 3/4 cup milk, the lemon juice, and eggs. Beat for 30 seconds, then scrape down the sides and bottom of the bowl with a rubber spatula and beat on medium speed for 1 minute. Add the warm water and the 2 teaspoons vanilla. Beat for 1 more minute.

Using a 1 1/2-ounce (3-tablespoon) ice cream scoop, scoop 24 mounds of batter 2 inches apart onto the prepared pans. Bake for 10 to 15 minutes, or until the center of each cake springs back to the touch. Remove from the oven and let cool completely on the pans. Use a spatula to transfer the cakes to a tray.

For the frosting: Using an electric mixer, beat the shortening and confectioners' sugar until blended. Gradually beat in the 1/4 cup milk and the 1/2 teaspoon vanilla. Beat until the mixture is light and fluffy.

Using a spatula, spread a thin layer of frosting onto the bottom of each cooled cake, then place a second cake on top, bottom side down. Dust with confectioners' sugar and serve.

Chef's Tip:
To make whoopie pies using another cake mix, you may need to cut back on the amount of liquid the recipe calls for so that the batter is slightly thicker.

BLUEBERRY COFFEE CAKE
MAKES ONE 9 BY 13-INCH CAKE

This moist, buttery coffee cake is packed with brown sugar and cinnamon and bursting with blueberries. It's the perfect complement to a steaming cup of morning coffee.

1/2 cup white rice flour
1/2 cup tapioca flour
1/2 cup potato starch
1/4 cup brown rice flour
1/4 cup sorghum flour
1 cup sugar
1 tablespoon baking powder
1 teaspoon salt
1 1/2 teaspoons xanthan gum
1/2 cup (1 stick) cold butter, cut into bits

1 cup milk
2 large eggs
1 teaspoon vanilla extract
2 cups fresh or frozen blueberries

TOPPING
1/3 cup packed light brown sugar
1/3 cup sugar
1 teaspoon ground cinnamon
1 tablespoon butter, melted

Preheat the oven to 325°F. Butter a 9 by 13-inch pan.

In a medium bowl, whisk together the white rice flour, tapioca flour, potato starch, brown rice flour, sorghum flour, the 1 cup sugar, the baking powder, salt, and xanthan gum. Using your fingers, a pastry blender, or two dinner knives, rub or cut the butter into the dry ingredients until it reaches the texture of coarse meal.

In a large bowl, whisk together the milk, eggs, and vanilla. Add the dry ingredients to the wet ingredients and whisk until thoroughly blended. Using a rubber spatula, fold in the blueberries and evenly spread the batter in the prepared pan.

For the topping: In a small bowl, blend together the brown sugar, the 1/3 cup sugar, the cinnamon, and melted butter. Sprinkle the topping evenly over the batter and bake for 50 to 55 minutes, or until a toothpick inserted in the center of the cake comes out clean. Remove from the oven and let cool completely on a wire rack. Cut into squares to serve.

SPICED PUMPKIN ROLL
SERVES 8 TO 10

This spicy pumpkin rolled cake with a cream cheese filling is my wife's favorite dessert. Gently roll the cake to ensure an even, rounded appearance.

1/4 cup white rice flour
1/4 cup brown rice flour
1/4 cup sorghum flour
1 teaspoon xanthan gum
3/4 teaspoon baking powder
1/2 teaspoon baking soda
1 teaspoon pumpkin pie spice
1/4 teaspoon ground cinnamon
1/2 teaspoon ground nutmeg
1/4 teaspoon salt
3 large eggs

1 cup sugar
2/3 cup canned solid-pack pumpkin
1/2 cup walnuts, chopped (optional)

FILLING
1 (8-ounce) package cream cheese, at
  room temperature
1 cup confectioners' sugar, sifted
6 tablespoons unsalted butter, at room temperature
1 teaspoon vanilla extract
Confectioners' sugar for dusting

Preheat the oven to 375°F. Butter a 10 by 15-inch jelly roll pan and line it with parchment paper. Butter the paper.

In a medium bowl, combine white rice flour, brown rice flour, sorghum flour, xanthan gum, baking powder, baking soda, pumpkin pie spice, cinnamon, nutmeg and salt. Stir with a whisk to blend.

Using an electric mixer, beat the eggs and sugar on medium speed until thick and creamy. Gradually beat in the pumpkin, then the flour mixture. Pour the batter into the prepared pan and spread evenly with a rubber spatula.

Sprinkle the batter with the walnuts and bake until the cake springs back when touched, about 15 minutes. Remove from the oven and let cool completely in the pan.

For the filling: Using an electric mixer, beat the cream cheese, confectioners' sugar, butter, and vanilla until smooth.

Carefully remove the cake from the pan by lifting the parchment paper and placing it, with the cake, on a work surface. Using a rubber spatula, evenly spread the cream cheese frosting over the cake.

To roll the cake, place it with one long side facing you. Beginning with that side, slowly roll the cake while peeling back the parchment paper. Try not to roll the cake too tightly or it may crack. After the cake is shaped like a jelly roll, wrap in plastic wrap and refrigerate for at least 2 hours or up to 1 day.

Unwrap the cake, dust with confectioners' sugar, and cut into slices to serve.

CARROT CAKE WITH CREAM CHEESE FROSTING
MAKES ONE 9-INCH CAKE

This dense, moist carrot cake, made with freshly grated carrots, raisins, and pecans and topped with a sweet cream cheese frosting, is absolutely amazing.

1 cup brown rice flour
1/2 cup white rice flour
1/4 cup tapioca flour
1/2 teaspoon xanthan gum
1 teaspoon baking soda
1 teaspoon baking powder
1/2 teaspoon salt
1 1/4 teaspoons ground cinnamon
1/2 teaspoon ground ginger
1/4 teaspoon ground nutmeg
1/2 cup (1 stick) unsalted butter, at room temperature
1/2 cup sugar
1/2 cup packed light brown sugar

2 large eggs
1/2 teaspoon vanilla extract
1 pound carrots, peeled and shredded (2 cups)
1/2 cup raisins
1/2 cup chopped pecans

CREAM CHEESE FROSTING
2 (8-ounce) packages cream cheese, at room temperature
1/2 cup (1 stick) unsalted butter, at room temperature
4 teaspoons vanilla extract
4 cups confectioners' sugar, sifted

Preheat the oven to 350°F and butter a 9-inch springform pan.

In a medium bowl, combine the brown rice flour, white rice flour, tapioca flour, xanthan gum, baking soda, baking powder, salt, cinnamon, ginger, and nutmeg. Stir with a whisk to blend.

Using an electric mixer on medium speed, cream together 1/2 cup of the butter and the sugars until light and fluffy. Beat in the eggs and vanilla, and then gradually beat in the dry ingredients to make a smooth batter. Stir in the carrots, raisins, and pecans just until blended.

Scrape the batter into the prepared pan and bake for 35 to 40 minutes, or until a toothpick inserted in the center comes out clean. Remove from the oven and let cool completely on a wire rack.

For the frosting: Using an electric mixer, beat together the cream cheese, the 1/2 cup butter, and the 4 teaspoons vanilla on medium speed. Add the confectioners' sugar and continue beating until the frosting is smooth and creamy.

Unmold the cake and place on a work surface. Cut the cake in half horizontally and separate the two layers. Place the bottom layer on a platter and spread with 3/4 cup frosting. Place the top layer on

CARROT CAKE WITH
CREAM CHEESE FROSTING (CONTINUED)

top and, using a rubber spatula or an icing spatula, spread the frosting over the top and sides of the cake smoothly and evenly. Using a pastry bag fitted with a star tip, pipe rows of stars across the top of the cake, creating a checkerboard effect. Place whole pecans in the squares between the piped rows and refrigerate the cake until serving. The cake can be refrigerated for up to 2 days. Cut into slices to serve.

CHAPTER 6

QUICK BREADS
BISCUITS
MUFFINS
BREAD STICKS

I hope that you enjoy making these wonderful biscuit, muffin, and bread stick recipes, and that ultimately, they will inspire you to create your own signature collection of gluten-free baked goods for you and your family to enjoy for years to come.

FLAKY BUTTERMILK BISCUITS
MAKES 12 BISCUITS

Also known as baking soda biscuits, these buttery morsels are delicious on their own or can be used to make the perfect strawberry shortcakes.

1 cup tapioca flour
1/2 cup sweet white rice flour
1/2 cup white rice flour
1/2 cup potato starch
1/2 cup cornstarch
1 1/2 teaspoons xanthan gum
4 teaspoons baking powder

1 1/2 teaspoons baking soda
1 teaspoon sugar
1 teaspoon salt
5 tablespoons vegetable shortening
4 tablespoons cold unsalted butter, cut into bits
1 1/2 cups buttermilk

Preheat the oven to 425°F. Butter a baking sheet.

In a medium bowl, combine the tapioca flour, sweet rice flour, white rice flour, potato starch, cornstarch, xanthan gum, baking powder, baking soda, sugar, and salt. Stir with a whisk to blend.

Using your fingers, a pastry blender, or two dinner knives, rub or cut the shortening and butter into the dry ingredients until the mixture is coarse and crumbly. Add the buttermilk and stir just until the dry ingredients are moistened.

Drop 1/4-cup mounds of dough 2 inches apart on the prepared pan. Bake for 10 to 12 minutes, or until golden brown. Remove from the oven and let cool slightly. Serve warm.

CHEDDAR AND CHIVE BISCUITS
MAKES 12 TO 15 BISCUITS

The mild, sweet onion flavor of the chives offsets the sharp Cheddar cheese, making these flaky biscuits a real treat. These are best straight from the oven.

1 cup brown rice flour
1/4 cup sweet rice flour
1/4 cup quinoa flour
1/4 cup tapioca flour
1/4 cup potato starch
1 1/2 teaspoons baking powder
1/4 teaspoon baking soda
3/4 teaspoon salt

1/2 teaspoon xanthan gum
3 tablespoons vegetable shortening
3 tablespoons cold unsalted butter
1 large egg, beaten
1 cup shredded sharp Cheddar cheese
1/4 cup minced fresh chives
1 cup buttermilk

Preheat the oven to 425°F. Butter a baking sheet.

In a medium bowl, combine the brown rice flour, sweet rice flour, quinoa flour, tapioca flour, potato starch, baking powder, baking soda, salt, and xanthan gum.

Using your fingers, a pastry blender, or two dinner knives, cut the shortening and butter into the flour mixture until the mixture is coarse and crumbly. Stir in the egg, cheese, and chives until blended. Stir in the buttermilk just until the ingredients are moistened.

Drop 1/4-cup scoops of dough 1 inch apart onto the prepared pan. Bake for 15 to 20 minutes, or until golden brown. Remove from the oven and let cool slightly on wire racks before serving.

Bacon, Cheddar, and Chive Biscuits:
Add 5 slices crisply cooked and crumbled bacon along with the cheese.

PARMESAN POPOVER BITES
MAKES 4 DOZEN BITES

These popover bites remind me of hot, buttery crescent rolls. Crispy on the outside yet light and airy on the inside, these are a delicious substitute for the dinner roll.

2 cups tapioca flour
1 cup sweet rice flour
1/2 cup potato starch
2 cups shredded Parmesan cheese

1 teaspoon salt
1 1/2 cups milk
3/4 cup canola oil
4 large eggs, beaten

Preheat the oven to 425°F. Butter two 24-cup mini muffin tins.

In a large bowl, combine the tapioca flour, sweet rice flour, potato starch, Parmesan cheese, and salt. Stir with a whisk to blend. Gradually whisk in the milk, oil, and eggs.

Pour the batter into a small pitcher and fill each muffin cup three-fourths full. Bake for 15 to 20 minutes, or until lightly golden brown. Remove from the oven and serve warm.

CORN BREAD
SERVES 10

Corn bread is a classic quick bread that can be difficult for the novice gluten-free chef to perfect. Using a coarsely ground cornmeal gives the bread a chewier texture and more interesting flavors.

1 1/2 cups coarsely ground yellow cornmeal
1 cup Authentic Foods Multiblend Gluten-Free Flour
1/4 cup sugar
1 teaspoon baking powder
1/2 teaspoon baking soda

1 teaspoon salt
1 large egg, lightly beaten
1 1/2 cups buttermilk
3/4 cup (1 1/2 sticks) unsalted butter, melted

Preheat the oven to 400°F. Butter a 10-inch square baking pan.

In a large bowl, combine the cornmeal, flour, sugar, baking powder, baking soda, and salt. In a medium bowl, combine the egg, buttermilk, and melted butter. Whisk to blend. Gradually add the wet ingredients to the dry ingredients, stirring just until moistened. Pour the batter into the prepared pan and bake for 25 to 30 minutes, or until golden brown.

Remove from the oven and let cool on a wire rack. Serve warm or at room temperature, cut into squares.

PECORINO PIZZA CRUST
MAKES TWO 12-INCH PIZZAS

After months of testing and tweaking, I finally developed this gluten-free pizza crust to the point of perfection. For me, the ultimate accolade was achieved when unsuspecting friends chose the gluten-free version as their favorite when this pizza was served with two "regular" pizzas ordered from our local pizza place. This will guarantee shouts of, "Mama Mia! Pizzeria!"

1 cup warm water (110°F)
1 package active dry yeast
1 cup sorghum flour
1/2 cup brown rice flour
1/2 cup white rice flour
1/4 cup tapioca flour, plus extra for dusting
1/4 cup potato starch
1/4 cup golden milled flaxseeds (page 24)
1/4 cup cornstarch
3 tablespoons dry milk powder

1 tablespoon sugar
2 teaspoons xanthan gum
1/4 teaspoon salt
1/2 cup grated pecorino romano or Parmesan cheese
1/2 cup shredded mozzarella cheese
5 cloves garlic, roasted (page 28)
2 tablespoons olive oil
1 large egg, lightly beaten
Pizza sauce, cheese, and toppings, as desired

In a small bowl, sprinkle the yeast over the warm water. In a food processor, combine the sorghum flour, brown rice flour, white rice flour, tapioca flour, potato starch, flaxseeds, cornstarch, milk powder, sugar, xanthan gum, salt, and pecorino and pulse until mixed. Blend in the mozzarella cheese and garlic, and then add the olive oil, egg, and yeast mixture, pulsing until a dough ball begins to form.

Transfer the dough to a pastry board lightly floured with tapioca flour. Divide the dough in half and form each into a ball. Place each ball of dough in an oiled bowl, and turn the dough to coat with oil. Cover with a damp towel or plastic wrap, and let rise in a warm place for 1 hour, or until the dough springs back when touched.

Preheat the oven to 500°F with a pizza stone on the bottom rack. Place a dough ball on the lightly floured (with tapioca flour) board and flatten the dough into a round, beginning in the center and working outward. Using a rolling pin, roll the dough from the center outward until the round is 12 inches in diameter. Roll and pinch the edges to make a rim. Lightly sprinkle a pizza peel or baking sheet with cornmeal and slowly slide it under the dough. Dough could also be rolled on a pizza peel, or formed into a pan.

Spoon 1/3 cup sauce, 1/3 cup cheese, and the desired toppings on top of the crust. Try not to overload the pizza with toppings, or you will end up with a soggy pizza.

PECORINO PIZZA CRUST (CONTINUED)

Transfer the pizza to the oven by carefully sliding it off the peel or pan onto the pizza stone. Bake for 15 to 20 minutes, until the crust is crisp and the cheese is lightly golden brown. While the pizza is baking, prepare the second pizza crust, using the same method.

Pecorino Bread Sticks:

Follow the instructions in the above recipe for preheating the oven and flattening the dough, but form the dough into an 8-inch square. Using a rolling pin, roll the dough to a 1/4-inch thickness. Using a knife, cut 1/2-inch-wide strips. Roll the dough into rounded sticks.

Dust a pizza peel or baking sheet with cornmeal and place the sticks on the pan. Brush the sticks lightly with melted butter, and sprinkle with your choice of sesame seeds, poppy seeds, grated Parmesan cheese, or kosher salt. Cover with a dry towel and let rise for 1 hour, or until the dough springs back when touched.

Gently slide the bread sticks off the peel or pan onto the pizza stone. Bake for 15 to 20 minutes, or until golden brown. Makes 2 dozen bread sticks.

Chef's Tip:

A preheated pizza stone is the key to making a crisp crust. But if you don't have one, simply bake the pizzas or bread sticks on a cornmeal-dusted baking sheet.

ZUCCHINI-SPICE BREAD
MAKES ONE 9 BY 5-INCH LOAF
SERVES 8 TO 12

The perfect recipe for using up the extra zucchini in your garden. This fragrant bread will stay moist for days.

1 cup brown rice flour
1/2 cup white rice flour
1/4 cup tapioca flour
1/2 teaspoon xanthan gum
1 teaspoon baking soda
1/2 teaspoon baking powder
1/2 teaspoon salt
1 1/4 teaspoons ground cinnamon

1/2 teaspoon ground ginger
1/4 teaspoon ground nutmeg
1/2 cup (1 stick) unsalted butter, at room temperature
1/2 cup sugar
1/2 cup packed light brown sugar
2 large eggs, lightly beaten
1/2 teaspoon vanilla extract
2 medium zucchini, shredded (2 cups)

Preheat the oven to 350°F. Butter a 9 by 5-inch loaf pan.

In a medium bowl, combine the brown rice flour, white rice flour, tapioca flour, xanthan gum, baking soda, baking powder, salt, cinnamon, ginger, and nutmeg. Stir with a whisk to blend.

Using an electric mixer on medium speed, cream together the butter and sugars until light and fluffy. Beat in the eggs and vanilla, then gradually beat in the dry ingredients just until combined. Stir in the zucchini.

Scrape the batter into the prepared pan, smooth the top with a rubber spatula, and bake for 55 to 60 minutes, or until a toothpick inserted into the center comes out clean. Remove from the oven and let cool on a wire rack for 15 minutes. Unmold and cut into slices to serve.

CRANBERRY-WALNUT BREAD
MAKES ONE 9 BY 5-INCH LOAF

A delicious bread to bake for the holidays and to give as a gift. Orange zest and cranberries give it color and a tart flavor.

1/2 cup sorghum flour
1/2 cup white rice flour
1/2 cup brown rice flour
1/4 cup tapioca flour
1 teaspoon xanthan gum
1 teaspoon baking soda
1/2 teaspoon baking powder
1/2 teaspoon salt

1/2 cup (1 stick) unsalted butter, at room temperature
1 cup sugar
3/4 cup freshly squeezed orange juice
2 large eggs, lightly beaten
1 teaspoon grated orange zest
1 cup fresh or thawed frozen cranberries, chopped
1/2 cup walnuts, chopped

Preheat the oven to 350°F. Butter a 9 by 5-inch loaf pan.

In a medium bowl, whisk together the sorghum flour, white rice flour, brown rice flour, tapioca flour, xanthan gum, baking soda, baking powder, and salt.

Using an electric mixer on medium speed, cream together the butter and sugar until light and fluffy. Beat in the orange juice, eggs, and orange zest. Gradually beat in the dry ingredients until a smooth batter forms.

Stir in the cranberries and walnuts. Pour the batter into the prepared pan and bake for 55 to 60 minutes, until a toothpick inserted in the center of the bread comes out clean. Remove from the oven and let cool on a wire rack for 15 minutes. Unmold and cut into slices to serve.

Cranberry-Walnut Muffins:
Scoop the batter into buttered muffin cups and fill each two-thirds full, sprinkle with sugar, and bake for 25 to 30 minutes. Makes 12 muffins.

CHOCOLATE CHIP— BANANA BREAD
MAKES ONE 9 BY 5-INCH LOAF

This is a favorite quick bread for many kids. The trick to making it highly moist and sweet is to use overripe bananas (the blacker, the sweeter.) If you don't have time to make this bread when the bananas are prime, freeze them in their skins, then thaw, peel, and mash when you are ready to begin.

1/2 cup chocolate chips
1/2 cup walnuts, chopped
1 cup white rice flour
1/4 cup brown rice flour
1/4 cup sorghum flour
1 teaspoon xanthan gum
1 teaspoon baking soda

1 teaspoon baking powder
1/4 teaspoon salt
1/2 cup (1 stick) unsalted butter, at room temperature
1 cup sugar
2 large eggs, beaten
1 1/2 teaspoons vanilla extract
1 cup mashed banana (about 2 medium bananas)

Preheat the oven to 350°F. Butter a 9 by 5-inch loaf pan.

In a small bowl, combine the chocolate chips and walnuts. Stir to mix. In a medium bowl, combine the white rice flour, brown rice flour, sorghum flour, xanthan gum, baking soda, baking powder and salt. Stir with a whisk to blend.

Using an electric mixer on medium speed, cream the butter and sugar together until light and fluffy. Add the eggs and vanilla, beating until thoroughly incorporated, and then mix in the mashed banana. Gradually beat in the dry ingredients until a smooth batter forms.

Pour one-third of the batter into the prepared pan and sprinkle in half of the nut mixture, followed by another one-third of the batter. Sprinkle with remaining nut mixture and the remaining batter. Smooth the top and bake for 50 minutes, or until a toothpick inserted in the center of the bread comes out clean. Remove from the oven and let cool for 15 minutes on a wire rack. Unmold and cut into slices to serve.

Chocolate Chip–Banana Muffins:
Fill 12 buttered muffin cups two-thirds full with the batter and bake for 25 to 30 minutes.

BLUEBERRY CRUMBLE MUFFINS
MAKES 12 MUFFINS

Try serving these blueberry muffins in the early morning, sliced, toasted, and spread with butter. No one will be late to breakfast!

1/2 cup sorghum flour
1/2 cup white rice flour
1/2 cup brown rice flour
1/4 cup tapioca flour
1 1/2 teaspoons baking powder
1 teaspoon xanthan gum
1/2 teaspoon salt
6 tablespoons butter, melted
1/2 cup sugar
1/2 cup packed dark brown sugar

1/2 cup milk
1 large egg
1 1/2 cups fresh or frozen blueberries

TOPPING
1/3 cup brown rice flour
1/2 cup sugar
1/4 cup packed light brown sugar
1/2 teaspoon ground cinnamon
2 teaspoons unsalted butter, melted

Preheat the oven to 400°F. Butter a 12-cup muffin pan. In medium bowl, combine the sorghum flour, white rice flour, brown rice flour, tapioca flour, baking powder, xanthan gum, and salt. Stir with a whisk to blend.

In another medium bowl, combine the 6 table-spoons melted butter, 1/2 cup sugar, the dark brown sugar, milk, and egg. Whisk to blend. Gradually whisk the dry ingredients into the wet ingredients until the batter is smooth. Fold in the blueberries, and scoop into the prepared muffin cups, filling each two-thirds full.

For the topping: In a small bowl, mix all the ingredients together until crumbly. Sprinkle on top of the muffins and bake for 25 to 30 minutes. Remove from the oven and allow to cool in the pan before unmolding and serving.

BANANA-CINNAMON NUT MUFFINS
MAKES 12 MUFFINS

The combination of sweet, ripe bananas and creamy buttermilk makes these muffins unique. Cinnamon and chopped pecans complement the flavors for a wonderful addition to your afternoon tea.

4 tablespoons butter, at room temperature
1/2 cup sugar
1 large egg
1 teaspoon vanilla extract
4 ripe bananas, peeled and cut into thin slices
1 cup buttermilk
3/4 cup sorghum flour
1/2 cup amaranth flour
1/4 cup sweet rice flour
1/4 cup potato starch
1/4 cup tapioca flour
2 teaspoons baking powder

1/2 teaspoon baking soda
1 teaspoon xanthan gum
1/2 teaspoon ground cinnamon
1/4 teaspoon salt
3/4 cup pecans, chopped

CRUMB TOPPING
1/3 cup brown rice flour
1/3 cup packed light brown sugar
1/2 teaspoon ground cinnamon
3 tablespoons cold butter

Preheat the oven to 350°F. Butter a 12-cup muffin pan.

Using an electric mixer on medium speed, cream together the butter, sugar, egg, and vanilla. Add the bananas and buttermilk, continuing to beat until smooth.

In a medium bowl, combine the sorghum flour, amaranth flour, sweet rice flour, potato starch, tapioca flour, baking powder, baking soda, xanthan gum, cinnamon, and salt. Stir with a whisk to blend.

Beat the dry ingredients into the creamed mixture until thoroughly blended. Fold in the pecans with a rubber spatula. Fill the muffin cups two-thirds full and set aside.

For the topping: In a medium bowl, combine the flour, brown sugar, and cinnamon. Using your fingers, a pastry blender, or two dinner knives, rub or cut in the butter until the mixture becomes coarse and crumbly. Sprinkle on top of the muffins and bake for 25 to 30 minutes, or until golden brown. Remove from the oven and allow to cool in the pan before unmolding and serving.

PUMPKIN NUT MUFFINS
MAKES 12 MUFFINS

Every October, my cousin Gary holds the annual family reunion on his apple farm in upstate New York. A large platter of these freshly baked pumpkin nut muffins are served alongside his hot apple cider—the perfect afternoon snack.

1/2 cup sorghum flour
1/2 cup brown rice flour
1/2 cup white rice flour
1/4 cup tapioca flour
1/2 teaspoon xanthan gum
1 teaspoon baking soda
1/2 teaspoon baking powder
1/2 teaspoon salt
1 teaspoon ground cinnamon
1/2 teaspoon ground ginger
1/4 teaspoon ground nutmeg

1/4 teaspoon ground allspice
1/2 cup (1 stick) unsalted butter, at room temperature
1 cup sugar
1 cup packed light brown sugar
2 large eggs, beaten
1 1/2 cups canned solid-pack pumpkin
1 cup pecans or walnuts, coarsely chopped

TOPPING
1/8 teaspoon ground cinnamon
1 tablespoon sugar

Preheat the oven to 350°F. Butter a 12-cup muffin pan.

In a medium bowl, combine the sorghum flour, brown rice flour, white rice flour, tapioca flour, xanthan gum, baking soda, baking powder, salt, the 1 teaspoon cinnamon, the ginger, nutmeg, and allspice. Stir with a whisk to blend.

Using an electric mixer on medium speed, cream the butter and sugars together until light and fluffy. Beat in the eggs and pumpkin, then gradually beat in the dry ingredients until a smooth batter forms. Stir in the walnuts.

For the topping: In a small bowl, stir the cinnamon and sugar together.

Fill the prepared muffin cups two-thirds full and sprinkle each muffin with a pinch of the topping. Bake for 30 to 35 minutes, or until a toothpick inserted into center of the muffins comes out clean. Remove from the oven and allow to cool in the pan before unmolding and serving.

CHAPTER 7

COOKIES SWEET BARS

One of my goals as a gluten-free cook was to create recipes for a variety of cookies that were easy to make, looked and tasted delicious, and held together as nicely as those made with wheat flour. This was an especially daunting task, given the fact that removal of gluten proteins from the baking process and the addition of gluten-free flours clearly affects the taste and texture of baking products. After a little research and many attempts and experimentations, I learned how to combine different gluten-free flours to reach my goal.

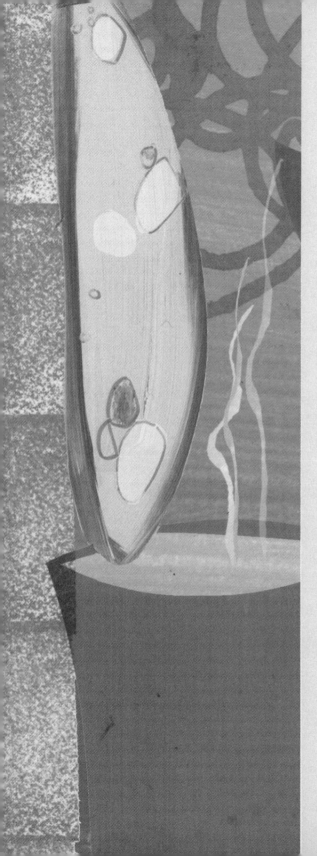

One challenge in gluten-free baking is that milder, blander flours, such as tapioca, white rice, potato starch, and cornstarch, when used on their own or combined incorrectly, tend to leave a slight aftertaste. However, when they are combined in the right proportions with more assertive flours, such as brown rice, sorghum, chestnut, or garbanzo, they work together to create a richer, cleaner, and more enjoyable taste.

Secondly, using the right binding agent makes a big difference in the quality of the final product. Starches or fibers such as xanthan gum or guar gum, combined with eggs, help to bind the flours and give cookie batters a consistency similar to those made with wheat flour.

Some of the following cookie and sweet bar recipes are naturally gluten free and don't require any substitutions or changes. Ground almonds, sugar, vanilla, and egg whites are the basis for the Almond Cookies, and the Chocolate Chip–Peanut Butter Cookies are simply made with peanut butter, eggs, sugar, and chocolate chips. I have also shared some recipes using commercially produced gluten-free cereals such as EnviroKidz Amazon Frosted Flakes, which make quick and easy Frosted Flake Bars.

Some other gluten-free baking tips to consider (for use in cookies, shortbreads, quickbreads, cakes, and muffins) include the following. To increase moisture, try using sour cream, yogurts, buttermilk, applesauce, maple syrup, fruit juices, or honey. To add new flavors, use chocolate chips, dried cranberries, fruit zests, coconut, raisins, nuts, peanut butter, vanilla, and spices such as cinnamon, nutmeg, ginger, and so on.

Although this chapter probably contains many of your favorite cookies, don't be afraid to experiment with that old family recipe that you haven't used lately because it contains gluten. By following the discussed guidelines, you may succeed in perfecting a new and better version, one that the whole family can enjoy.

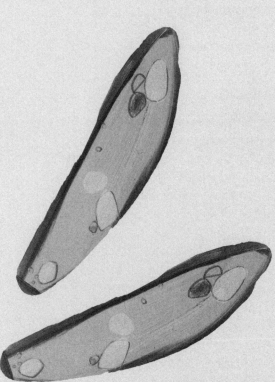

ALMOND COOKIES
MAKES 2 DOZEN COOKIES

These classic Italian cookies are made by grinding almonds and sugar into a meal that is then folded into beaten egg whites. The end result is delightful cookies: light, chewy, nutty, and sweet.

1 3/4 cups sliced almonds, toasted (page 27)
1 cup sugar
2 large egg whites

1 teaspoon vanilla extract
Sliced almonds, for garnish
Confectioners' sugar, for dusting

Preheat the oven to 325°F. Line two baking sheets with parchment paper.

Place the toasted almonds and 1/2 cup of the sugar in a food processor and process until finely ground.

Using an electric mixer on low spead, beat the egg whites until foamy, then increase the speed to medium-high and beat until soft peaks form. Gradually beat in the remaining 1/2 cup sugar, then the vanilla, continuing to beat until stiff, glossy peaks form.

Using a rubber spatula, carefully fold the almond mixture into the egg whites until just blended. Spoon the mixture into a pastry bag fitted with a 1/2-inch plain tip and pipe 2-inch rounds 1 inch apart on the prepared pans. Press a sliced almond into the center of each round and bake for 12 to 15 minutes, or until golden brown. Using a thin metal spatula, transfer the cookies to a wire rack to cool completely. Dust with confectioners' sugar to serve.

SPICED OATMEAL–RAISIN COOKIES
MAKES 4 DOZEN COOKIES

These childhood favorites combine an aromatic, flavorful mixture of spices with a special blend of gluten-free flours, oats, and plump raisins. They are the perfect complement to a glass of cold milk.

1/2 cup brown rice flour
1/2 cup sweet rice flour
1/4 cup tapioca flour
1/4 cup potato starch
1 teaspoon ground cinnamon
1 teaspoon ground nutmeg
1 teaspoon ground ginger
1/2 teaspoon ground allspice
1 teaspoon xanthan gum

1/2 teaspoon baking soda
1/2 teaspoon salt
1 cup (2 sticks) unsalted butter, at room temperature
1 cup packed light brown sugar
1 cup sugar
1 large egg
1 teaspoon vanilla extract
3 cups gluten-free quick oats (see Note)
1 cup raisins

Preheat the oven to 375°F. Butter two baking sheets.

In a medium bowl, combine the brown rice flour, sweet rice flour, tapioca flour, potato starch, cinnamon, nutmeg, ginger, allspice, xanthan gum, baking soda, and salt. Stir with a whisk to blend.

Using an electric mixer on medium speed, cream together the butter and sugars until light and fluffy. Beat in then egg and vanilla, and then scrape down the sides and bottom of the bowl with a rubber spatula. On low speed, gradually add the dry ingredients to make a dough. Stir in the oats and raisins.

Drop heaping tablespoonfuls of dough 2 inches apart on the prepared pans. Bake for 10 to 12 minutes, or until golden brown. Remove from the oven and let cool for 5 minutes. Transfer the cookies to wire racks to cool completely.

Note:
Make sure you use oats that are certified gluten-free, meaning that they are inspected and noncontaminated. Companies such as Gifts of Nature, Bob's Red Mill, Cream Hill Estates, and Gluten Free Oats implement specific measures to avoid cross-contamination from wheat to oats in planting, growing, harvesting, and processing procedures. For more on this, see page 20.

Oatmeal–Chocolate Chip–Raisin Cookies:
Reduce the raisins to 1/2 cup and add 1/2 cup chocolate chips.

CHOCOLATE CHILLER DROPS
MAKES 2 DOZEN COOKIES

Need a quick dessert? These rich and delicious no-bake drops go from the microwave to the fridge and then right onto your plate.

6 ounces semisweet chocolate, finely chopped
2 ounces unsweetened chocolate, finely chopped
2/3 cup sweetened condensed milk

2/3 cup gluten-free white chocolate chips
1/2 cup sliced almonds, finely chopped

Line a baking sheet with parchment paper and lightly coat the paper with cooking spray.

In a microwavable bowl, combine the semisweet and unsweetened chocolate. Microwave on high for 1 minute, and let rest for 2 to 3 minutes. Microwave on high again for 1 minute, and then remove and stir for 15 to 20 seconds. Place back in the microwave oven on high for 30 seconds more, and then stir until smooth.

Stir in the condensed milk until thoroughly combined, and then stir in the chocolate chips and nuts. Drop heaping teaspoonfuls of dough 1/2 inch apart on the prepared pan. Refrigerate until firm, about 1 hour. Serve at room temperature.

ALMOND BISCOTTI
MAKES 3 DOZEN COOKIES

Biscotti is Italian for "twice baked." These crisp cookies originated in Tuscany and are usually served with coffee or wine.

2 large eggs
1 1/2 teaspoons vanilla extract
2 1/4 cups Authentic Foods Multiblend
   Gluten-Free Flour
 1 1/2 teaspoons baking powder

3/4 teaspoon salt
6 tablespoons unsalted butter, at room temperature
3/4 cup sugar
1 cup sliced almonds, toasted (see page 27)

Preheat the oven to 325°F. Butter a baking sheet.

In small bowl, beat together the eggs and vanilla. In a medium bowl, combine the flour, baking powder, and salt. Stir with a whisk to blend.

Using an electric mixer on medium speed, beat the butter and sugar together until light and fluffy. Gradually beat in the egg mixture, then the dry ingredients. Stir in the almonds until incorporated.

On a pastry board lightly dusted with tapioca flour, divide the dough in half. Roll each half into a log 2 inches wide and 10 inches long. Transfer to the prepared pan, leaving a 4-inch space between the logs for spreading. Bake for 40 minutes, or until firm to the touch. Remove from the oven and let cool for 10 to 15 minutes on a wire rack.

Transfer the logs to a cutting board and, using a serrated knife, cut into 1/2-inch diagonal slices Place on the baking pan again and bake for 25 minutes, or until dry and slightly brown. Remove from the oven and transfer the cookies to wire racks to cool completely.

White Chocolate–Cranberry Biscotti:
In place of almonds, add 1 cup dried cranberries and 3/4 cup white chocolate chips.

Chocolate Chip–Almond Biscotti:
Reduce the almonds by 1/2 cup and add 1/2 cup chocolate chips.

Walnut Biscotti:
Replace the almonds with 1 cup toasted walnuts.

Anise-Flavored Biscotti:
Add 1 teaspoon anise extract and 1 teaspoon of aniseeds.

CHOCOLATE CHIP— PEANUT BUTTER COOKIES
MAKES 2 DOZEN COOKIES

Chocolate and peanut butter are every kid's favorite. This classic combination that cannot go wrong is an ode to the peanut butter cup.

1 cup chunky peanut butter
1 large egg, beaten
3/4 cup plus 2 tablespoons sugar

1/2 cup chocolate chips
1/2 cup Reese's Pieces

Preheat the oven to 350°F. Butter a baking sheet.

In a medium bowl, combine all the ingredients and stir to blend. Refrigerate for 5 to 10 minutes, or until firm.

Using a teaspoon, scoop the dough into 1/2-inch balls and place 2 inches apart on the prepared pan. Flatten with a fork and bake for 10 minutes, or until lightly browned. Allow to cool on a baking sheet for 5 minutes, then transfer to a wire rack and let cool completely.

CHOCOLATE ALMOND COOKIES
MAKES 2 DOZEN COOKIES

Beaten egg whites make this a light and airy cookie, while the cocoa adds a hint of chocolate. These are the perfect treats for tea parties and bridal showers.

1 cup sliced almonds, toasted (see page 27), plus more for garnish
1/2 cup sugar
1 tablespoon unsweetened cocoa powder

2 tablespoons confectioners' sugar
2 large egg whites
Pinch of cream of tartar
1 teaspoon almond extract

Preheat the oven to 350°F. Line a baking sheet with parchment paper.

In a food processor, combine the 1 cup toasted almonds and 1/4 cup of the sugar. Pulse until finely ground. Transfer to a bowl. Sift the cocoa and confectioners' sugar into the bowl and stir to blend.

Using an electric mixer, beat the egg whites and cream of tartar on low speed until foamy, then increase the speed to medium-high and beat until soft peaks form. Gradually beat in the remaining 1/4 cup sugar and continue to beat until stiff, glossy peaks form. Using a rubber spatula, fold in the almond extract, then the almond sugar 1/2 cup at a time until just blended.

Spoon the mixture into a pastry bag fitted with a 1/2-inch plain tip and pipe 2-inch mounds 1 inch apart on prepared pan. Press a sliced almond into the center of each mound and bake for 12 to 15 minutes, or until golden brown. Remove from the oven and, using a thin metal spatula, transfer the cookies to wire racks to cool completely.

LUSCIOUS LEMONY CHESTNUT BARS
MAKES 16 BARS

An original blend of sweet, tart, and nutty: a tangy taste of heaven wrapped up in one bar.

1/2 cup brown rice flour
1/4 cup tapioca flour
1/4 cup chestnut flour
1/4 cup potato starch
1/4 cup sugar
1/4 teaspoon salt
6 tablespoons cold butter, cut into small pieces

3/4 cup sugar
2 large eggs
1 tablespoon grated lemon zest
3 tablespoons freshly squeezed lemon juice
1/2 teaspoon baking powder
Pinch of salt
Confectioners' sugar, for dusting

Preheat the oven to 350°F. Line an 8-inch square pan with aluminum foil and butter the foil.

In a food processor, combine the brown rice flour, tapioca flour, chestnut flour, potato starch, 1/4 cup sugar, and the salt. Whirl to blend. Add the butter and process until a fine meal forms. Press evenly into the bottom and sides of the prepared pan to form a crust. Bake for 15 minutes, or until slightly golden.

Meanwhile, prepare the filling: In a food processor, combine the 3/4 cup sugar, the eggs, lemon zest and juice, baking powder, and salt. Process to blend. Pour into the hot crust and bake for 20 minutes, or until set. Remove from the oven and let cool completely on a wire rack. Cut into 16 squares, remove from the pan, and dust with confectioners' sugar to serve.

FROSTED FLAKE BARS
MAKES 12 BARS

In this unique twist on the crispy rice and marshmallow treat, corn flakes, chocolate chips, raisins, and nuts combine to make a satisfying snack or dessert. I use EnviroKidz Amazon Frosted Flakes in this recipe to achieve the perfect crunch.

4 cups mini marshmallows
4 tablespoons butter
1/3 cup creamy peanut butter

7 1/2 cups gluten-free frosted flake cereal
1 cup chocolate chips, raisins, or nuts (optional)

Lightly butter a 9 by 13-inch cake pan and set aside.

In a large microwavable bowl, combine the marshmallows and butter and microwave on high for 3 minutes. Stir in the peanut butter until smooth. Stir in the frosted flakes and chocolate chips until the frosted flakes are completely coated. Using a buttered rubber spatula, spread and press the mixture evenly into the pan. Let cool completely, then cut into 12 bars to serve.

WOW! BROWNIES
MAKES 24 BARS

Authentic Foods makes a multiblend flour mix combining brown rice flour, sweet rice flour, tapioca starch, cornstarch, potato starch, and xanthan gum. I always keep a bag of this flour on hand for use when pinched for time. These brownies are as good as any can get, and with each bite I have to say, Wow!

3/4 cup (1 1/2 sticks) butter
4 ounces unsweetened (baking) chocolate
2 cups sugar
3 large eggs

1 teaspoon vanilla extract
1 cup Authentic Foods Multiblend Gluten-Free Flour
1 cup walnuts (optional)

Preheat the oven to 350°F. Butter an 8 by 11-inch baking pan.

In a large microwavable bowl, microwave the butter and chocolate on high for 2 minutes. Stir with a wooden spoon and then microwave for 1 more minute. Stir until the chocolate is completely melted and smooth. Stir in the sugar, eggs, and vanilla. Gradually stir in the flour until blended, then the walnuts.

Pour into the prepared pan and spread evenly with a rubber spatula. Bake for 40 to 45 minutes, or until a toothpick inserted in the center comes out clean. Remove from the oven and let cool completely in the pan. Cut into bars to serve.

CHOCOLATE-OATMEAL-PEANUT SQUARES
MAKES 24 BARS

These stove-top cookies are an easy, delicious treat. Dense and chewy, they're perfect for an afternoon snack or a child's lunchbox.

2 cups sugar
1/2 cup milk
1/2 cup (1 stick) butter
1/2 cup unsweetened cocoa powder

1/2 cup chunky peanut butter
1 teaspoon vanilla extract
1 1/2 cups gluten-free quick oats

Butter an 8-inch square baking pan.

In a medium saucepan, combine the sugar, milk, butter, and cocoa. Bring to a boil over medium-high heat and cook for 2 to 3 minutes, stirring constantly. Remove from the heat and stir in the peanut butter and vanilla until blended. Stir in the oats and pour into the prepared pan. Let cool, then refrigerate for 3 to 4 hours, or until chocolate sets. Cut into bars to serve.

CHOCOLATE CHIP COOKIES
MAKES ABOUT 4 DOZEN COOKIES

A special blend of sorghum flour, garbanzo flour, and cornstarch make these chocolate chip cookies even better than the classic originals. You won't believe it until you taste them. Serve with a tall glass of cold milk.

1 cup sorghum flour
3/4 cup garbanzo (chickpea) flour
1/2 cup potato starch
1/4 cup cornstarch
1 teaspoon baking soda
1 teaspoon baking powder
1 teaspoon salt
1 teaspoon xanthan gum

1 cup (2 sticks) butter, at room temperature
3/4 cup sugar
3/4 cup packed light brown sugar
2 large eggs
1 teaspoon vanilla extract
2 cups chocolate chips
1 cup walnuts, chopped (optional)

Preheat the oven to 375°F. In a small bowl, combine the sorghum flour, garbanzo flour, potato starch, cornstarch, baking soda, baking powder, salt, and xanthan gum. Stir with a whisk to blend.

In a separate bowl, using an electric mixer on medium speed, cream together the butter and sugars. Beat in the eggs and vanilla, and then gradually beat in the flour mixture until blended, stopping to scrape down the sides and bottom once or twice. Stir in the chocolate chips and walnuts.

Drop rounded tablespoons or dough 2 inches apart onto ungreased baking sheets. Bake for 10 to 12 minutes, or until golden brown. Remove from the oven and let cool completely on the pan before serving.

Variation:

Substitute 2 1/2 cups of Authentic Foods Multiblend Gluten-Free Flour for the sorghum flour, garbanzo flour, potato starch, and cornstarch.

RASPBERRY- COCONUT BARS
MAKES 24 BARS

A personal favorite: these buttery, nut-crusted bars are layered with raspberry preserves and toasted coconut.

1 1/2 cups sweetened coconut
1/2 cup brown rice flour
1/4 cup tapioca flour
1/4 cup potato starch
1/4 cup walnuts, chopped
1/2 cup packed light brown sugar

1/4 cup sugar
1/2 teaspoon xanthan gum
1/4 teaspoon salt
6 tablespoons cold butter, cut into small pieces
3/4 cup raspberry preserves

Preheat the oven to 375°F. Butter an 8 by 11-inch baking pan. Spread the coconut evenly on a baking sheet and toast in the oven for 8 to 10 minutes, turning once, until golden brown. Remove from the oven and let cool completely.

In a food processor, combine the brown rice flour, tapioca flour, potato starch, walnuts, brown sugar, sugar, xanthan gum, and salt. Whirl to blend. Add the butter and process until a fine meal forms. Transfer the flour mixture to a bowl and stir in the toasted coconut. Remove ¾ cup of the mixture and reserve for the topping.

Press the remaining flour mixture firmly and evenly onto the bottom and sides of the prepared pan to form a crust. Spread the raspberry preserves evenly on top of the dough and sprinkle with the reserved flour mixture. Bake for 20 to 25 minutes, or until topping is lightly browned. Remove from the oven and let cool completely on a wire rack before cutting into 24 bars.

NUTTY BRITTLE
MAKES 12 OUNCES

This easy nut brittle recipe can be made in a matter of minutes, right in the microwave. You can use either peanuts or cashews—both make for a crunchy, candied delight.

1 cup sugar
1/2 cup light corn syrup
1/8 teaspoon salt
1 cup skinned raw peanuts or cashews

1 teaspoon unsalted butter
1 teaspoon vanilla extract
1 teaspoon baking soda

Butter an 11 by 17-inch baking sheet.

In a large microwavable bowl, combine the sugar, corn syrup, salt, and peanuts. Microwave on high for 4 minutes, stir the mixture, and then microwave on high another 5 minutes or until golden in color. Stir in the butter and vanilla and microwave for 1 more minute. Stir in the baking soda and microwave for 1 more minute. Pour onto the prepared pan and, using a rubber spatula, quickly spread the mixture 1/4 inch thick. The mixture will not fill the pan. Let cool completely before breaking into pieces.

CHOCOLATE FUDGE BARS
MAKES 12 BARS

The sumptuous layers of bittersweet chocolate and milk chocolate fudges make these bars a chocolate-lover's dream.

1 (11 1/2-ounce) package bittersweet chocolate chips (see Note)
1 (14-ounce) can sweetened condensed milk
2 tablespoons heavy cream or milk

2 teaspoons vanilla extract
1 cup chopped walnuts (optional)
1 (11 1/2-ounce) package milk chocolate chips (see Note)

Line the inside of a 9-inch square pan with aluminum foil and butter the bottom and sides of the foil.

In a medium saucepan, combine the bittersweet chocolate chips, 2/3 cup of the condensed milk, 1 tablespoon of the cream, and 1 teaspoon of the vanilla. Heat over low heat until melted and stir until smooth. Remove from the heat and stir in 1/2 cup of the walnuts, if using. Spread evenly into the prepared pan.

In a separate saucepan, combine the milk chocolate chips with the remaining condensed milk, 1 tablespoon cream, and 1 teaspoon vanilla. Remove from the heat and stir in the remaining walnuts, if using.

Spread the milk chocolate fudge evenly over the bittersweet fudge in the pan and refrigerate for at least 3 hours. Unmold the fudge onto a cutting board, peel off the foil, and cut into squares.

Note:

Make sure to read labels on chocolate chips and bars to ensure that they are truly gluten-free. Some companies will state that their chocolate is made in a facility that also packages wheat-based products, which makes cross-contamination possible.

MAPLE-PECAN BARS
MAKES 24 BARS

Several years ago, Tom Hurst, owner of the Hurst Family Farm, spent a day teaching me the art of maple sugaring. We emptied numerous buckets from his maple trees and led a team of oxen pulling the sap in a large wagon. After slowly cooking down the sweet liquid, we had some of New England's richest maple syrup. It was the inspiration that led me to create these incredible bars.

PASTRY CRUST
1/2 cup brown rice flour
1/4 cup tapioca flour
1/4 cup potato starch
1/4 cup pecans
1/2 cup packed light brown sugar
1/4 cup sugar
1/2 teaspoon xanthan gum
1/4 teaspoon salt
6 tablespoons cold butter, cut into small pieces

FILLING
1/3 cup pure maple syrup
1/3 cup packed light brown sugar
1/4 cup heavy cream
2 tablespoons unsalted butter
1 3/4 cups pecans, coarsely chopped
1/2 teaspoon vanilla extract

Confectioners' sugar, for dusting

Preheat the oven to 375°F. Line an 8-inch square baking pan with aluminum foil and butter the bottom and sides of the foil.

For the crust: In a food processor, combine the brown rice flour, tapioca flour, potato starch, pecans, the 1/2 cup brown sugar, the sugar, xanthan gum, and salt. Whirl to blend. Add the butter and blend until a fine meal forms. Press the crust mixture evenly over the bottom and sides of the prepared pan. Bake for 20 minutes, or until the edges of crust begin to brown.

Meanwhile, make the filling: In a medium saucepan, combine the maple syrup, the 1/3 cup brown sugar, the cream, and butter. Bring to a boil over medium heat, stirring to dissolve the sugar, and cook for 2 minutes. Remove from the heat and stir in the pecans and vanilla. Pour into the hot crust and bake for 10 minutes, or until the filling bubbles in the center.

Remove from the oven and let cool completely in the pan. Unmold the cake and remove the foil. Place the cake on a cutting board and cut into 24 squares. Dust with confectioners' sugar to serve.

PUMPKIN COOKIES WITH PENUCHE FROSTING
MAKES 6 DOZEN COOKIES

These pumpkin cookies are coated with a thin frosting called penuche that lends a sugary, fudgelike flavor.

1/2 cup brown rice flour
1/2 cup sweet rice flour
1/2 cup tapioca flour
1/2 cup potato starch
1 teaspoon baking soda
1 teaspoon baking powder
1 teaspoon ground cinnamon
1/2 teaspoon ground nutmeg
1/2 teaspoon salt
1 cup (2 sticks) butter, at room temperature
1/2 cup sugar

1/2 cup packed light brown sugar
1 cup canned solid-pack pumpkin
1 large egg
1 teaspoon vanilla extract
1 cup chopped pecans or walnuts

PENUCHE FROSTING
3 tablespoons butter
1/2 cup packed brown sugar
1/4 cup milk
2 cups confectioners' sugar, sifted

Preheat the oven to 350°F. Butter baking sheets.

In a medium bowl, combine the brown rice flour, sweet rice flour, tapioca flour, potato starch, baking soda, baking powder, cinnamon, nutmeg, and salt. Stir with a whisk to blend.

Using an electric mixer on medium speed, cream the butter, sugar, and 1/2 cup brown sugar together until creamy. Beat in the pumpkin, egg, and vanilla, then gradually beat in the dry ingredients. Stir in the nuts.

Drop teaspoonfuls of batter 2 inches apart on the prepared pans. Bake for 10 to 12 minutes, until firm to the touch. Remove from the oven and let the cookies cool for 5 minutes on a pan, then transfer to a wire rack.

For the frosting: In a small saucepan, combine the butter and the 1/2 cup brown sugar. Bring to a boil over medium-high heat, stirring to dissolve the sugar. Cook and stir for 1 minute, or until slightly thickened. Transfer to a small bowl and let cool for 15 to 20 minutes. Using a whisk, break up the mixture and gradually whisk in the milk. Whisk until smooth. Gradually whisk in the confectioners' sugar until smooth and spreadable. Frost the cookies and serve.

CHOCOLATE-DIPPED PEANUT BUTTER BALLS
MAKES 4 DOZEN COOKIES

My sister-in-law, Darlene, is an avid baker who loves to experiment with gluten-free recipes. Whenever Darlene comes over for dinner, she is expected to bring a plate of her famous peanut butter balls. There is a running family challenge to try to eat just one!

1 cup (2 sticks) butter
1 cup chunky peanut butter (not natural style)
2 1/4 cups confectioners' sugar

1 3/4 cups crushed gluten-free vanilla animal cookies
1 cup semisweet chocolate chips
2 tablespoons vegetable shortening

Line an 11 by 17-inch baking sheet with waxed paper and set aside.

In a medium saucepan, combine the 1 cup butter and the peanut butter. Warm over low heat and stir until melted. Stir in the sugar and cookie crumbs. Remove from the heat and let cool. Cover and refrigerate for 30 minutes, or until set.

Form the dough into 1-inch balls and place on the prepared pan. Refrigerate for 1 hour or until set.

In a small pan, stir the chocolate chips and the 2 tablespoons of shortening over low heat until melted. Dip the balls in the chocolate mixture and return to the baking sheet. Refrigerate until the chocolate sets, about 1 hour.

NO-BAKE INDOOR S'MORES
MAKES 12 BARS

The original s'more was a campfire-toasted marshmallow topped with milk chocolate and sandwiched between two graham crackers. These indoor s'mores are made in the microwave and formed into bars.

6 cups miniature marshmallows
1 1/2 cups chocolate chips
1/4 cup light corn syrup

5 tablespoons butter
1 teaspoon vanilla extract
8 cups gluten-free honey-coated cornflakes

Butter a 9 by 13-inch pan. In a large microwavable bowl, combine the marshmallows, chocolate chips, corn syrup, and butter. Microwave on high for 2 to 3 minutes, stirring after each minute until smooth. Stir in the vanilla. Add the cereal and toss quickly until evenly coated.

Using a rubber spatula, press the mixture evenly into the prepared pan. Let stand at room temperature for at least 1 hour, or until firm. Cut into bars to serve.

CHOCOLATE-DRIZZLED MACAROONS
MAKES 2 DOZEN COOKIES

Macaroons were supposedly invented in the late 1700s in an Italian monastery. The monks came up with this delicious, sweet, and chewy coconut confection.

2 1/2 cups sweetened flaked coconut
3/4 cup sugar
Pinch of salt

3 large egg whites
1/2 teaspoon vanilla extract
4 ounces semisweet chocolate, chopped

Preheat the oven to 375°F. Line two baking sheets with parchment paper.

In a medium bowl, combine the coconut, sugar, and salt. Stir to blend.

In a medium bowl, beat the egg whites with a fork until foamy. Stir in vanilla and then add the egg mixture to the coconut mixture, stirring until the ingredients are evenly moistened.

Drop tablespoonfuls of batter 2 inches apart onto the prepared pan. Bake for 12 to 15 minutes, or until golden brown. Remove from the oven and let cool completely on the pans.

Melt the chocolate in a small saucepan over medium-low heat until smooth. Using a fork, drizzle the chocolate over the macaroons. Let stand until the chocolate is set. Using a thin metal spatula, carefully remove the macaroons from the pan to serve.

HONEY NUT CEREAL BARS
MAKES 12 BARS

I use a honey nut cereal made by Glutino in this recipe, but these crunchy, nutty stove-top bars can also made with any favorite nongluten cereal you prefer.

1/2 cup sugar
1/2 cup honey

1/2 cup natural smooth peanut butter
3 cups honey nut cereal

Butter a 9 by 13-inch pan and set aside.

In a medium saucepan, combine the sugar and honey. Bring to a boil over medium-high heat, stirring to dissolve the sugar. Remove from the heat and stir in the peanut butter until blended. Stir in the cereal until completely coated. Using a rubber spatula, spread the mixture evenly in the prepared pan and let cool completely. Cut into squares to serve.

ALMOND FUDGE BARS
MAKES 24 BARS

Just one tablespoon of chestnut flour adds a hint of roasted nut flavor to these delicate, sweet bars.

CRUST
30 Glutino Chocolate Wafers
2 tablespoons light brown sugar
1 tablespoon chestnut flour
Pinch of salt
4 tablespoons unsalted butter, melted

FILLING
3/4 cup (1 1/2 sticks) unsalted butter,
  at room temperature
3/4 cup packed light brown sugar
6 tablespoons corn syrup
3 cups sliced almonds
3 tablespoons heavy cream
2 ounces unsweetened chocolate, chopped

Preheat the oven to 350°F. Line an 8-inch square pan with aluminum foil and butter the bottom and sides of the foil.

For the crust: In a food processor, combine the wafers, the 2 tablespoons brown sugar, the chestnut flour, and salt. Pulse to grind. Add the melted butter and process until a fine meal forms. Press the mixture evenly and firmly over the bottom and sides of the prepared pan to make a crust. Refrigerate for 15 minutes, and then bake for 10 minutes, or until lightly browned

Meanwhile, prepare the filling: Combine the 3/4 cup butter, 3/4 cup brown sugar, and corn syrup in a medium saucepan. Bring to a boil over medium-high heat, stirring constantly. Cook and stir for 1 minute, then stir in the nuts and cream. Cook stirring for 2 minutes, or until slightly thickened. Remove from the heat and stir in the chocolate until melted. Pour into the hot crust and bake until bubbly in the center, 12 to 15 minutes.

Remove from the oven and let cool completely. Unmold the cake, remove the foil, and cut into 24 bars.

JACKER CRACK BARS
MAKES 12 LARGE BARS

This easy snack is perfect for children's parties. The caramel-covered popcorn and peanut treat is reminiscent of the baseball park classic.

8 cups popped popcorn (about 1/3 cup unpopped)
3/4 cup peanuts (optional) roasted, unsalted
1 cup packed light brown sugar
1/4 teaspoon salt

1/2 cup (1 stick) butter
3 tablespoons light corn syrup
1/2 teaspoon vanilla extract
1/2 teaspoon baking soda

Preheat the oven to 350°F. Line an 8 by 11-inch pan with aluminum foil and butter the bottom and sides of the foil.

In a large bowl, combine the popcorn and peanuts, if using, and set aside.

In a medium saucepan, combine the brown sugar, salt, butter, and corn syrup. Bring to a boil over medium heat, stirring constantly. Cook for 3 minutes without stirring, then remove from the heat and stir in the vanilla and baking soda. Pour over the popcorn and peanuts and gently stir until evenly coated. Pour into the prepared pan. Using a buttered spatula, spread out evenly. Bake for 20 minutes, or until set and crisp. Remove from the oven and let cool completely.

Invert the pan onto a cutting board and carefully remove the aluminum foil. Cut into squares to serve. Store leftovers in an airtight container for up to 3 days.

CHOCOLATE-NUT BUSTER BARS
MAKES 12 BARS

These tasty treats of sweetened cereal, peanut butter, chocolate chips, and peanuts are more like a candy bar than a cookie. A children's sticky-finger favorite!

6 cups gluten-free Rice Chex cereal
1 cup semisweet chocolate chips
2/3 cup unsalted roasted peanuts
1/2 cup packed light brown sugar

1/2 cup sugar
1 cup light corn syrup
1 cup natural peanut butter

Butter a 9 by 13-inch pan and set aside. In a medium bowl, combine the cereal, chocolate chips, and peanuts.

In a medium saucepan, combine the brown sugar, sugar, corn syrup, and peanut butter. Stir over medium heat until melted and smooth. Pour the peanut butter mixture evenly over the Rice Chex mixture and toss until the cereal is coated. Pour into the prepared pan. Using a buttered spatula, gently spread the mixture evenly. Let cool completely before cutting into bars.

CHAPTER 8

PUDDINGS
MOUSSES
COBBLERS

Puddings, mousses, and cobblers can become safe and delicious "comfort food" desserts in the gluten-free kitchen. In this chapter, you'll find excellent recipes for rich and delicious puddings and mousses made with cornstarch or eggs. Some of the recipes incorporate whole eggs, whereas others require use of egg yolks or whites separately. Egg yolks produce a thickening quality that adds richness and density to a dessert, whereas egg whites make a mousse light and airy. In my Indian Pudding recipe, I rely on cornmeal to slowly absorb the liquid, which results in a satisfying and rich New England favorite.

BUTTERSCOTCH PUDDING
SERVES 6

A melding of dark brown sugar, butter, and vanilla makes this a rich and creamy butterscotch pudding. One bite and you will never eat the store-bought version again.

2 tablespoons butter
1 1/4 cups evaporated milk
3/4 cup packed dark brown sugar
2 cups cream or milk
3 tablespoons cornstarch
1/8 teaspoon salt
3 large egg yolks
1 1/2 teaspoon vanilla extract

TOPPING
3/4 cup heavy cream
3 tablespoons confectioners' sugar
1/4 cup chopped Heath Toffee Bar

In a small saucepan, melt the butter over medium heat. Add 1/4 cup of the evaporated milk and the brown sugar and cook, stirring constantly, until the mixture begins to boil. Cook for 30 seconds, constantly stirring, then remove from the heat and set aside.

In a medium saucepan, heat the cream over medium-high heat until tiny bubbles begin to form around the edge of the pan; remove from the heat and set aside.

In a medium bowl, combine the remaining 1 cup evaporated milk, the cornstarch, salt, and egg yolks. Whisk until blended. Whisk into the hot cream, and then whisk in the brown sugar mixture. Return the pan to medium heat and bring to a boil for 1 minute. Remove from the heat and stir in the vanilla. Spoon the mixture into 4-ounce custard cups or a large bowl. Cover by pressing plastic wrap directly onto the surface. Let cool, then refrigerate for at least 4 hours or up to 2 days.

For the topping: In a deep bowl, combine the cream and confectioners' sugar. Beat until soft peaks form. Spoon the whipped cream on top of the pudding and sprinkle with the chopped candy.

CREAMY VANILLA PUDDING

SERVES 6 TO 8

For a quick summertime dessert, use martini glasses and build layers with this smooth vanilla pudding and fresh berries. Garnish with whipped cream and a mint leaf—oooohhhh, sooooo good.

2/3 cup sugar
1/4 cup cornstarch
1/4 teaspoon salt
4 cups cream or milk

4 large egg yolks, lightly beaten
4 tablespoons butter, at room temperature
4 teaspoons vanilla extract

In a medium saucepan, combine the sugar, cornstarch, and salt. Stir with a whisk to blend. In a medium bowl, combine the cream and egg yolks and whisk until blended. Stir into the sugar mixture and cook over medium heat, stirring constantly, until the mixture simmers and begins to thicken, 2 to 3 minutes. Cook for 1 minute, constantly stirring, then remove from the heat and stir in the butter and vanilla.

Pour into individual custard cups and cover with plastic wrap pressed directly onto the surface of the pudding. Refrigerate for at least 3 hours or up to 2 days.

INDIAN PUDDING
SERVES 8 TO 10

After sampling the incredible Indian pudding served to me in a quaint New England restaurant, I set out to create a version that could be enjoyed by everyone on a chilly winter night in front of a crackling fire.

5 1/2 cups whole milk
1 cup packed light brown sugar
2/3 cup stone-ground yellow cornmeal
2 tablespoons light molasses
2 tablespoons honey
1 large egg

1 teaspoon ground ginger
1 teaspoon ground cinnamon
1/4 teaspoon salt
4 tablespoons unsalted butter
1/4 teaspoon vanilla extract
Vanilla ice cream, for serving

Preheat the oven to 325°F. Butter a 9 by 13-inch baking dish.

In a heavy, medium saucepan, combine the milk, brown sugar, cornmeal, molasses, honey, egg, ginger, cinnamon, and salt. Whisk to blend. Cook, whisking frequently, over medium-high heat for about 20 minutes, until the mixture thickens but can still can be poured. Remove from the heat and whisk in the butter and vanilla.

Pour into the prepared dish and bake until golden brown and the center is firm, 2 to 2 1/2 hours. Remove from the oven and let cool for 10 minutes, then scoop into bowls and serve topped with vanilla ice cream.

NO-BAKE RICE PUDDING
SERVES 6 TO 8

This no-bake version of an old-fashioned favorite is prepared completely on the stove top. It's the easiest way to enjoy a sumptuous bowl of creamy rice pudding.

1 1/2 cups water
1 cup uncooked long-grain white rice
1 cup sugar
3 tablespoons cornstarch
1/4 teaspoon salt

6 cups milk or heavy cream
2 large eggs, beaten
1 1/2 teaspoons vanilla extract
5 tablespoons butter
1/2 teaspoon ground cinnamon

In a saucepan, bring the 1 1/2 cups water to a boil. Stir in the rice, cover, decrease heat, and simmer for 15 minutes until all the water is absorbed.

In small bowl, combine the sugar, cornstarch, and salt. Stir with a whisk to blend.

In medium saucepan, combine the milk, eggs, and vanilla. Whisk to blend. Place over medium-high heat and whisk in the sugar mixture. Whisking constantly, bring the milk mixture to a low simmer and stir in the cooked rice. Continue stirring until the mixture boils and thickens, 5 to 10 minutes.

Remove from the heat, stir in the butter, and pour into a 9 by 13-inch pan. Sprinkle with cinnamon and cover the pudding with plastic wrap by pressing it directly onto the surface of the pudding. Refrigerate for at least 4 hours or up to 2 days.

Raisin Rice Pudding:
Stir in 3/4 cup raisins before pouring into the pan.

MIMI'S CHOCOLATE MOUSSE
SERVES 4 TO 6

Dinner at my father's house means his wife Mimi's famous chocolate mousse is soon to follow. The best way to describe it is creamy, rich, and chocolaty.

4 ounces semisweet chocolate, chopped
4 teaspoons unsalted butter
2 large egg yolks (see Note)

4 large egg whites
4 teaspoons sugar

In a double boiler over barely simmering water, melt the chocolate with the butter. Remove from the heat and let cool slightly. In small bowl, beat the egg yolks until pale and frothy, then stir into the chocolate mixture.

Using an electric mixer, beat the egg whites until soft peaks form. Add the sugar and beat until stiff, glossy peaks form. Fold the egg whites into the chocolate mixture and spoon the mousse into individual ramekins. Cover and refrigerate for at least 3 hours or up to 2 days.

Note:
Consuming raw or undercooked eggs may put children, the elderly, pregnant women, and people with compromised immune systems at risk for salmonella.

FRESH BERRIES WITH ZABAGLIONE
SERVES 4 TO 6

Zabaglione is an Italian custard made from egg yolks, sugar, and Marsala wine. Dolloped over fresh berries alongside a scoop of vanilla ice cream, it makes a special dessert. Using Grand Marnier liqueur gives the zabaglione a wonderful orange flavor. Both Marsala wine and Grand Marnier are gluten free.

2 cups fresh strawberries, hulled and sliced
1 cup fresh blueberries
1 cup fresh raspberries
8 large egg yolks

1/2 cup sugar
1/2 cup dry Marsala, or 1/3 cup Grand Marnier
1 pint vanilla ice cream

In a medium bowl, combine the berries and toss to mix.

In a medium stainless-steel bowl, whisk together the egg yolks and sugar until blended. Set the bowl over a saucepan filled with 2 inches of simmering water. Gradually whisk in the Marsala and continue to whisk constantly until the mixture becomes thick and creamy, about 5 minutes. The mixture should form smooth mounds when spooned.

Scoop the vanilla ice cream into bowls or glasses, spoon the berries over the ice cream, and pour the warm zabaglione over the top. Serve at once.

VANILLA CARAMEL FLAN
SERVES 8

One of the perks of being a chef is the opportunity it affords to meet people from all over the world and to learn the customs and tastes of other cultures. I recently worked with a woman from the Dominican Republic named Maura, who shared with me the intricate art of making the perfect flan.

3/4 cup sugar
3 large eggs
1 (12-ounce) can evaporated milk

1 (14-ounce) can sweetened condensed milk
1 teaspoon vanilla extract

Preheat the oven to 350°F. In small, heavy saucepan, stir the sugar over medium-low heat until it turns a light brown caramel color, 8 to 10 minutes. Pour the caramel into a 9-inch round cake pan and tilt the pan to evenly coat the bottom and sides.

In large bowl, combine the eggs, evaporated milk, condensed milk, and vanilla. Whisk until blended. Pour over the caramel in the pan and set the pan in a baking pan. Place in the oven and add hot water to the baking pan to come halfway up the sides of the cake pan. Bake for 55 minutes, or until a knife inserted into the center of the flan comes out clean. Remove from the oven and let cool completely on a wire rack. Cover and refrigerate overnight.

To serve, run a butter knife around the edges to loosen the flan. Place a plate on top of the pan and quickly invert to unmold the flan, allowing any remaining caramel to drizzle over it. Cut into wedges to serve.

RICOTTA CREAM BERRY TRIFLE
SERVES 8 TO 10

Serving this amazing trifle in a large glass bowl displays the colorful layers of strawberries, blueberries, and sweetened white ricotta cheese filling. It's a Fourth of July picnic crowd-pleaser.

3/4 cup arrowroot cookies
3/4 cup walnuts
2 (15-ounce) containers ricotta cheese
2 cups confectioners' sugar
1 teaspoon vanilla extract
2 cups heavy cream

2 cups fresh blueberries
4 cups fresh strawberries, hulled and thinly sliced,
     plus 2 whole strawberries for garnish
1 cup miniature chocolate chips

For the topping: In a food processor, pulse the cookies and walnuts until finely ground.

Using an electric mixer on medium speed, beat together the ricotta cheese, sugar, and vanilla until smooth and creamy. In a deep bowl, beat the heavy cream until soft peaks form. Using a rubber spatula, fold the whipped cream into the ricotta cheese mixture.

In an 8-cup glass bowl, spread one-fourth of the cheese filling and layer with the blueberries. Repeat with one-fourth of the filling, followed by the sliced strawberries, then another one-fourth of the filling, followed by chocolate chips. Spread the remaining filling on top, sprinkle with the crumb topping, and garnish with the whole strawberries. Cover and refrigerate for at least 3 hours or up to 1 day.

PEACH COBBLER WITH SWEET CRUMBLE TOPPING
SERVES 6 TO 8

Sink your teeth into fresh, sweet peaches sprinkled with cinnamon sugar and topped with a buttery batter and chopped pecans. Served with a scoop of vanilla ice cream, this is a scrumptious summertime dessert.

1/4 cup sugar
1 teaspoon ground cinnamon
1 teaspoon cornstarch
8 peaches, peeled, pitted, and thinly sliced (see Note)
1/2 cup brown rice flour
1/2 cup amaranth flour
1 teaspoon baking powder
1/2 teaspoon baking soda
1/4 cup sugar

4 tablespoons cold unsalted butter, cut into small pieces
2/3 cup buttermilk
1/2 teaspoon vanilla extract
1/2 cup pecans, chopped
Vanilla ice cream, for serving

Preheat the oven to 400°F. Butter a 9 by 13-inch baking dish.

In small bowl, combine the sugar, cinnamon, and cornstarch. Stir with a whisk to blend. Place the sliced peaches in the prepared dish and sprinkle with the sugar mixture until evenly coated. Bake for 10 minutes.

While the peaches are baking, make the topping: In a medium bowl, combine the brown rice flour, amaranth flour, baking powder, baking soda, and sugar. Stir with a whisk to blend. Using your fingers, a pastry cutter, or two dinner knives, rub or cut the butter into the dry ingredients until the mixture is coarse and crumbly. Stir in the buttermilk, vanilla, and pecans, mixing just until a soft batter forms.

Remove the baking dish from the oven and drop spoonfuls of the topping on top of peaches. Bake for 20 minutes, or until lightly browned. Remove from the oven and let cool slightly. Serve with vanilla ice cream.

Chef's Tip:
To peel the peaches, cut an X into the skin on the bottom of each peach. Blanch the peaches in a large pot of boiling water for 45 to 50 seconds. Using a slotted spoon, transfer the peaches to a bowl of ice water for 30 seconds. Peel off the loosened skin with a paring knife.

CHAPTER 9

A CHEF'S PERSPECTIVE ON EATING OUT

In my travels as a gluten-free chef, I do quite a bit of consulting with individuals, school systems, universities, catering facilities, and private restaurants. Over the past five years, there has been a remarkable increase in the number of people diagnosed with celiac disease. Very often, the diagnosing gastroenterologist explains the disease well to the patient, but subsequently sends the person back out into the world amid a sea of hidden gluten sources. Most newly diagnosed patients are confused or a bit scared, and many start off with very limited diets, fearing they can only eat chicken, fruits, and vegetables. This is now very far from the truth, however, and there is no reason for fear, deprivation, or even avoidance of restaurants or wedding receptions. Being successful on a gluten-free diet just requires education through valid and trustworthy sources, access to good ingredients and recipes, and a willingness to explain to others in a clear and concise manner what the diet entails. It also requires the discipline to avoid the processed, gluten-filled foods that are always available at arm's length, and to have the necessary (and tasty) alternatives on hand—or waiting for you at your favorite restaurant—so that there will be no digestive regrets to ruin the next day.

COLLEGE DINING

Watching your son or daughter depart for college can be stressful enough without having to worry whether he or she can eat safely in the dining halls. This anxiety can be easily eliminated by contacting the dining services department, either the semester or summer before arrival, or as soon as possible after a diagnosis has been made, if your student is already on campus. Usually, a meeting will be arranged on site with you, the student, the dining facility manager, and a registered dietitian, as well as a dining hall chef who can answer any questions pertaining to the gluten-free menu on campus. Most colleges and universities are now already aware of celiac disease, and many have a variety of gluten-free options available on a daily basis. Most universities will also already have distributors in place to provide gluten-free breads, pastas, muffins and snacks, and so on. Given enough notice, your son or daughter's favorite items will be there, stored aside, and labeled, if necessary, on his or her arrival.

RESTAURANT AND CATERED DINING

Dining out with loved ones or friends should be an enjoyable experience, one we relish or look forward to as a special treat. For the person newly diagnosed with celiac disease, dining out can be a daunting prospect, but this can be remedied by taking a few easy steps. The first is simply to call the restaurant before your arrival, speak directly with the manager of the facility, and explain what your dietary needs are and when you will be dining. This is especially important when it comes to high-end restaurants or catered functions/wedding receptions, and so on, where there may be a limited menu. I cannot stress enough that this phone call is not a bother or inconvenience to the management or kitchen staff. In fact, because of the competitive nature of the restaurant industry, most establishments will welcome a call that gives them advance notice, so they can prepare as well as possible. Always remember that you are the consumer in a customer service–driven industry, and that most places are going to want to meet your needs, to keep your business or garner new business by word of mouth.

If you cannot or do not call ahead, there is still no need to panic. Upon arriving at the restaurant, ask to speak directly to the manager on duty, and explain as clearly as possible what it means to be wheat/gluten intolerant and how your food choices may have to be adjusted. (Some diners carry small cards available from various celiac organizations that explain fully and concisely the disease, ingredient and preparation restrictions, and alternatives. These are invaluable tools to hand to the manager and chef of any restaurant.) Speaking directly with the manager is always the best approach in an unfamiliar restaurant. This is simply because the manager acts as a liaison between the customer, chef, and all the individuals preparing and serving the food to your table. He or she should be able to explain

the situation to the staff so that you do not have to repeat yourself to four or five different employees. This also helps to eliminate some of the possible "minor" errors that can end up jeopardizing your health. For example, the busy waitress who runs back to the chef to ask if the chicken and rice dish has any wheat, may get a cursory "rice doesn't have wheat" from an overloaded cook. She returns to your table relaying that your dinner choice is safe. However, nobody checked to see whether the chicken stock that rice was boiled in does or does not contain gluten. Having a true understanding of the "back of the house" when dining in a restaurant is important. "Back of the house" refers to the kitchen, a formal title for "organized chaos." This is where your food, along with another three hundred or so meals, will be prepared, in the same space within a few hours' time. Making sure that the team realizes the grave nature of your disease can help them slow down and pay attention to the "minor" ingredients that really do matter.

Another important restaurant dining issue is that of cross-contamination. Questions invariably arise: Are they using the same cutting board to cut bread and then prepare your vegetables? Are they thickening their sauces with flour and then using the same sauté pan to cook your "gluten-free" entrée? Are those gluten-free French fries prepared in the same oil as the breaded onion rings? Most kitchens are required to maintain strict health standards, and no staff deliberately wants to make someone sick. Although I can't speak for all restaurants, many typically use different cutting boards (sometimes color coded) for different tasks. They also always have clean spoons, ladles, tongs, and pans all within reach. Gluten-free meals can be prepared separately and safely to reduce any chance of cross-contamination. You have a much better chance of obtaining a noncontaminated, gluten-free meal once a manager or waitperson stresses the importance to the back of the house. Offering to answer any questions regarding ingredients or preparation for the staff may also be helpful.

Many restaurants, especially the larger chains, are now offering gluten-free menus, available on request. This is just the beginning of a new industry that is guaranteed to take off as the number of gluten-intolerant people increases and more owners and managers are made aware of their needs. International trends are setting the stage, and many metropolitan areas, including Boston, New York, and Chicago, are already advertising gluten-free bakeries, pizzerias, and restaurants for your enjoyment.

ABOUT THE AUTHOR

Robert Landolphi is a 1991 graduate of Johnson and Wales University with a bachelor of arts degree in culinary arts and food service management. He also completed a certified culinary arts instructor program at Central Connecticut State University. Rob has enjoyed a variety of food-related occupations, including several years as a wedding coordinator/banquet manager at Glastonbury Hills Country Club, and owner and operator of the Sugar Shack Bakery in Storrs, Connecticut. He currently serves as a certified culinary arts instructor and the culinary operations manager with the University of Connecticut.

Rob is a member of the National Association of College and University Food Services, the American Culinary Federation, Slow Food International, and the National Restaurant Association. Rob has entertained audiences all over New England with his unique cooking style, personality, and down-to-earth yet informative demonstrations.

Rob's media credits include producing and hosting the *Mangia Radio* show at 91.7 FM-WHUS, and writing and hosting a cooking show called *Food for the Journey*. He has appeared on the Food Network's *How Do You Iron Chef?* promotion program while hosting the University of Connecticut's Annual Culinary Olympics, and on the new cable food program *Boy Meets Still*. Rob has also appeared on CBS Sports and WTNH News programs. He has made guest appearances on numerous *Food Talk* radio programs, and has shared recipes and industry food trend information with many magazines and newspapers.

Rob is married and has two young sons. He was introduced to the gluten-free lifestyle in the year 2000, when after a lengthy illness, his wife was finally diagnosed with celiac disease. Since that time, he has made it a personal mission to create and perfect gluten-free recipes that will satisfy even the harshest of critics, including those who do not need to be wheat- and gluten-free, but love his food anyway.

www.glutenfreechefrob.com

RESOURCES

Celiac Organizations

American Celiac Disease Alliance
www.americanceliac.org

Canadian Celiac Foundation
www.celiac.ca

Celiac Disease Foundation (CDF)
www.celiac.org

Celiac.com: Celiac Disease and
  Gluten-Free Diet Information
www.celiac.com

Gluten Intolerance Group (GIG)
www.gluten.net

Celiac Sprue Association/USA, INC (CSA)
www.csaceliacs.org

Gluten Free Culinary Productions, Inc.
www.theglutenfreelifestyle.com

National Foundation for Celiac
  Awareness (NFCA)
www.celiacawareness.org

Raising Our Celiac Kids (R.O.C.K.)
www.celiackids.com

The Gluten Free Chef
www.glutenfreechefrob.org

Magazines and Newsletters

Gluten-Free Living Magazine
www.glutenfreeliving.com

Living Without
www.livingwithout.com

Gluten-Free Food Distributors

Against the Grain Gourmet
www.againstthegraingourmet.com

Arrowhead Mills
www.arrowheadmills.com

Authentic Foods
www.authenticfoods.com

Barbara's Bakery
www.barbarasbakery.com

Bard's Tale Beer
www.bardsbeer.com

Bob's Red Mill Natural Foods
www.bobsredmill.com

Chebe Bread
www.chebe.com

Cream Hill Estates
www.creamhillestates.com

Dowd & Rogers
www.dowdandrogers.com

Ener-G Foods
www.ener-g.com

Erewhon/US Mills
www.usmillsinc.com

Food for Life
www.foodforlife.com

Foods by George
www.foodsbygeorge.co

Glutenfreeda
www.glutenfreeda.com

Gluten Free Foods
www.glutenfree.com

Gluten Free Mall
www.glutenfreemall.com

Gluten Free Oats
www.glutemfreeoats.com

Gluten-Free Pantry/Glutino USA
www.glutenfreepantry.com

Glutano
www.glutano.com

Glutino
www.glutino.com

Gillian's Foods
www.GilliansFoods.com

Grainless Baker
www.grainlessbaker.com

Health Valley Company
www.healthvalley.com

Hodgson Mill
www.Hodgsonmill.com

Kinnikinnick Food
www.kinnikinnick.com

Lundberg Family Farms
www.lundberg.com

Mary's Gone Crackers
www.marysgonecrackers.com

McCormick & Company
www.mccormick.com

Midel's
www.midelcookies.com

Namaste Foods
www.namastefoods.com

Nature's Path Foods
www.naturespath.com

Pamela's Products
www.pamelasproducts.com

Perky's 100% Natural
www.perkysnaturalfoods.com

Tinkyada
www.tinkyada.com

Wild Oats Markets
www.wildoats.com

Whole Foods Market
www.wholefoodsmarket.com

Wyman's Blueberries
www.wymans.com

Celiac Support Groups in the United States
www.enabling.org/ia/celiac/groups/
    groupsus.html

Dining Information
Bob and Ruth's GF Dining & Travel Club
www.bobandruths.com

Triumph Dining
www.triumphdining.com